BEYOND THE OHP

BEYOND THE OHP

A PRACTICAL GUIDE TO USING TECHNOLOGY IN WORSHIP

JACKIE SHEPPARD

First published in 2002 by Spring Harvest Publishing Division
and Authentic Lifestyle

08 07 06 05 04 03 02   7 6 5 4 3 2 1

Autentic Lifestyle is an imprint of Authentic Media
P.O. Box 300, Carlisle, Cumbria, CA3 0QS, UK
and Box 1047, Waynesboro, GA 30830-2047
www.paternoster-publishing.com

British Library Cataloguing in Publication Data

A catalogue record for this book is available from the British
Library

ISBN 1-85078-454-X

Cover design by Diane Bainbridge
Printed in Great Britain by
Cox and Wyman, Cardiff Road, Reading

Contents

Acknowledgements

With my thanks to:

The entire Baptist Assembly Technical Team for being such fun to work with. But, especially Steve Cayley, Andy Voyce (my co-producer) and Graham Preston (from Sound Foundation). Extra thanks to Steve Cayley for his help in checking for technical errors! Any that remain are mine. Extra thanks too to Andy Voyce for use of his 'Fred' story.

Darrell Jackson for introducing me to PowerPoint® in the first place

Dennis Choy at North Coast Community Church, Vista, California

Jean Smith at Milton Baptist Church, Weston-Super-Mare

Simon Hammond at Guisley Baptist Church, North Yorkshire

Simon Carver at South Oxford Baptist Church, Oxford

David Coffey for the illustration from *Romans* and for teaching me about team leadership

Ben Fortescue for the PowerPoint® illustrations.

Eddie Askew for permission to use his paintings – again.

Mum and Dad

And, finally, Jo Peacock for being a brilliant researcher and great fun to go rafting with. Next time, it's your turn to fall in!

Jackie Sheppard

Introduction

This book is offered as a guide to those churches wanting to use some of the new technology available (computer graphics, videos, lighting, etc) in their worship. I offer it out of the experience of producing events that involve the use of technology as an aid to worship. Over the last few years I have been involved in the production of the Annual Baptist Assembly and other Baptist events. The Assembly attracts around 2500 Baptists to venues around the country. We have worked in venues such as the Wembley Conference Centre, the Bournemouth International Centre, Plymouth Pavilions and the Norbreck Castle Hotel in Blackpool. It has become a technically demanding and challenging exercise. Every main session will involve some kind of visual presentation, or a video clip, or an audio presentation – some sessions will involve a combination of all of these. Lights, sound and vision all have to be co-ordinated – to say nothing of the people participating!

At the Assembly in 2001 held in Blackpool, some members of the technical team held a seminar for churches wanting to use technology in worship. One of the, perhaps inevitable, questions was 'how could churches replicate what we do at an Assembly?' There is no easy answer to that. The Assembly requires a production team of sixteen people and a great investment of resources. Not many churches could replicate that. But there are presentation principles that are the same whether you are producing a worship service for 50 people, 500, or 5000.

This is not a 'technical' book for the experts. I have tried to avoid any jargon words and where they are unavoidable, I have attempted to explain them.

This book may be too simplistic for some. But I hope that others will be helped by it. Occasionally I will make reference to useful websites. The difficulty with websites is that many disappear or change addresses so my apologies if you try to follow a link that no longer exists.

This book aims to give some guidance on how to use the technology available to us effectively. It provides case studies from within both the United Kingdom and the United States of America.

American churches tend to be much larger than their British counterparts, better staffed and better resourced. Many of them have been using technology in their services for many years. The opportunities afforded to the churches in America by a more localised television network mean that many are used to producing material week in and week out of broadcast standard. I offer the American case studies not as something to aspire to, but rather as something to learn from.

There are some do's and don'ts listed.

I don't hold myself up as an expert. Neither do I hold the Baptist Assembly up as a perfect example of how technology should be used but I will use it as illustrative examples at times because it is what I know. I will also use examples from the churches I have visited in both the UK and in the United States. This is not because they are the only churches using the technology but again because they provide examples from my own experience.

Nearly all of us who work on the Assembly Technical Team have 'day' jobs. The Assembly is an extra for us. What we have learned, we have learned through hands-on experience. But, we are willing to have a go, to use the technology to help people worship in different ways. I hope that this book will help you to have a go too.

CHAPTER 1

The Multi-media Age and the Changing Face of Church

The experience of going to church is changing. Walk into many churches today and you will find one or a combination of the following in use:

- projectors
- television cameras
- lighting systems
- sound systems.

Churches are using technology to help in getting across the message of the gospel. Today's congregations often expect it. We live in a multi-media age with access to twenty-four-hour news, information, instant messaging and electronic mail. Why should the experience of going to church be different?

Jesus used the means of communication pertinent to his audience. He told stories. He used examples and illustrations from everyday life: fishing, agriculture, the vineyard. He used the dominant cultural themes of the day to explore the message. Although we know this to be the case, sometimes we are given reminders. Stephen Rand, during his time as Director of Communications for Tear Fund, recalls how he was travelling down a road in Ethiopia in the darkness. Occasionally they would come across herds of animals on the road. The animals were herds of sheep and goats, and occasionally they would be a mixed herd. The response of the animals varied to the oncoming vehicle. The goats would do the sensible thing and make a run for it, whilst the sheep waited for one sheep to take the initiative for them all to follow. When the vehicle came upon a mixed flock the result was unpredictable – which animal's reaction would dominate the rest of the herd? Suddenly, Stephen saw Matthew 25 and Jesus' separation of the sheep and the goats in a whole new light. '… the basis of that separation was not by how they looked, but by how they responded …' (*Guinea Pig for Lunch*, Stephen Rand). Jesus knew his audience and he knew the most appropriate form of communication with which to communicate.

Today the dominant forms of communication are the television, radio, movies, music and the Internet. The predominant forms are visual. Even the Internet is a highly visual medium.

Some might argue that our experience of church should be 'different', set apart from the world. They would say by turning our churches into the equivalent of a TV studio we are in danger of losing the sense of majesty and awe, of the 'differentness'. Or that the projection of hymn/song words means we no longer have the words in our hands to study and reflect upon as we sing them. Or, watching the preacher with an image projected on to the big screen behind turns it from being a spiritual moment to a television performance.

But, if Jesus were here today doubtless he would relate to the culture of the day and make use of the technology available to explain and explore his message. The church has a unique opportunity to use the technology, to explore in new and exciting ways the 'old' stories of the gospel, to help a more sophisticated audience see afresh the truth of the message.

Furthermore, our audience may now expect it of us. I offer the following story which was told to me about a couple who sat at home one Sunday evening watching the BBC television programme, *Songs of Praise*. It was exciting and made the experience of attending church seem lively and fun. The next Sunday they decided to attend a church near to them. Unfortunately, the service was anything but lively and fun. They left, disillusioned, probably never to darken the doors of a church again.

It is a tragedy that people often see the church as boring and its presentation of poor quality – stuck in an earlier century. We should strive to be known as the place of excellence. There should be no 'second best'. Technology can help us to produce that which is exciting and dramatic. The technology alone can't do it. But *we* can, if we use the technology to best effect. That does not mean that everything we do has to be perfect. There is a difference between striving for excellence and perfectionism. The Oscar-winning film director Steven Soderbergh once said, 'Energy is more important than perfection … things that are alive have flaws.' Perhaps one of the strangest things about our use of technology in worship is that, if it is done well, it becomes almost invisible.

The ministry of celebration arts

Churches *are* using the technology. They look to the example of churches like Willow Creek Community Church, near Chicago, and see how they utilise multi-media to great effect. They want to replicate it – but how? There are few churches within the UK that can match the resources of a Willow Creek. We can learn from the larger churches how to use the technology and adapt it to our own situation and to match our own resources. We may not have enormous resources but our use of multi-media is really only bound by our own imagination and creativity. I have visited churches where I have cringed at the use of the technology and others where I have been inspired by it. Presentations on the big screen that have words and images flying in from all directions with multi-coloured backdrops are not necessarily helpful. Songs, where the words build one at a time, or the different lines fly in from alternate sides of the screen are a distraction. The technology should be there as an aid to worship. It is not a demonstration of the talents of those using it.

Read Acts 9:36–42. Peter is called to the house of Tabitha, a woman described as 'always doing good and helping the poor'. Tabitha dies but Peter raises her from the dead. The crunch of the passage for me is in v.42 because the news becomes known and people 'believed in the Lord'. It does not say, 'people believed in Peter'. What a humble spirit Peter must have had. Having raised somebody from the dead he points only to Jesus. However good our creative talents and skills are, if they don't help point people towards Jesus then we are not using them correctly and we may need to examine our own motives.

Having said that, we need to recognise the ministry of the 'techie'. Too often I hear people wax lyrical on the ministry of worship leaders, dramatists, musicians, and the preacher. But what about the ministry of the person on the sound desk, the person behind the video camera, the person on the lighting desk, the person sat at the computer? In America many churches have recognised the importance of the audio-visual and created the role of 'Minister for Celebration Arts'. This is the person who co-ordinates the work of the technical team. It is a recognition that the technician, or 'techie', is an artist and has just as much of a ministry as anybody else.

You need to determine what your particular gifting is. Are you a creative person? Are you a technical person? It is not necessarily the case that somebody who is competent technically will be a creative genius and vice versa. We need to find the right balance of technical and creative competence.

Using technology can also provide an opportunity to encourage young people to become involved. Often they are far more technically competent than the older generation. If young people are to be encouraged to participate it must not be at the expense of their spiritual development. Technology can become an all-consuming thing. Technicians in church are perhaps rather good at placing a low importance on spiritual matters. 'Hey, we're too busy being practical!' But, if every Sunday you are pressing buttons with no time to listen to the teaching what is happening to your spiritual life?

Computers are not necessarily the preserve of the younger generation. At the 2000 Baptist Assembly we experimented with 'broadcasting' our main sessions over the Internet. At that particular Assembly, Graham Kendrick was a guest worship leader on the Saturday evening. Unknown to him, the Assembly band had prepared a musical tribute for the evening. We later heard that Graham's 81-year-old father had been very moved by the tribute as he sat at home watching and listening on his computer. Often it is the older generation that has both the disposable income and the time to invest in the technology. The technical side can provide a great opportunity for young and old to work together.

If you are the lone person in a technical team you have my admiration and my sympathy. As with anything else, there is nothing like being a part of a team to aid creativity. As part of the Baptist Assembly production team I know that I am not the most technically competent person – that's why we have a Technical Consultant on the team. My task is to pull the creative threads together. I might have an idea for a video sequence but task somebody who is more competent than I am at video editing to actually produce it.

Just as Jesus had his team of supporters/assistants, so you will need yours. A good team supports and encourages one another and provides a substitute for when you go down with the 'flu! There's more on working as a team later.

What do we mean by worship?

The subtitle of this book is 'A Practical Guide to Using Technology in Worship' and without getting into any arguments I need to explain what I mean by worship. I have sat in some services where either the minister or worship leader says, 'Now let us worship God together' which roughly translated means, 'Let's all stand and sing a hymn and/or choruses'. I believe that everything we do in church is part of our worship so in this book you can take it to mean the **whole** service. We will also look at how churches can use the Internet to expand their worship outside the walls of the church, which will inevitably lead to a wider discussion of the use of the Internet.

Whatever you want to use the technology for – remember your main aim should always be for that transformational moment in people's lives. The technology is merely a tool to be used to support and complement the service. It can be a medium for the message, it is not **the** message. You are a part of a team, a team that needs to work together with a common goal. Your ministry is no more or less valid than that of anybody else. But lives are changed through the ministry of worship and preaching so your expertise can be used of God to heighten that audio-visual experience which is a work of the Holy Spirit.

CHAPTER 2

Converting Your Church

It may be that you are considering introducing technology into your worship. First things first – decide what you want and why you want it. It might be helpful to actually write down a mission or vision statement for your multimedia ministry. It might be along the lines of the following from Olive Baptist Church, Pensacola, Florida:

> The purpose of the Olive Baptist Church Media Ministry is to conceptualise and create progressive, culturally accurate media that:
>
> O enhance worship
> O act as an instrument for evangelism
> O support discipleship
> O serve ministry.
>
> We will accomplish the task by providing and maintaining an infrastructure that allows the processing of information and by acting as a communication

conduit between the staff, church members, our
community and the world.

(Vision Statement of Olive Baptist Church Media
Ministry, quoted in 'The Making of a Media Ministry'
by Allen Hendrix, Director of Media Ministries at
Olive Baptist Church. This article appeared in
Technologies for Worship Magazine Online.)

Or, it might be along the lines of the following:

We consider the technical team's ministry to be the
supporting of the messages that are produced within
this church. We will always strive to produce our creative and technical best as an offering to our brothers
and sisters within the church, to our visitors, and to
God. We will work with the leadership of the church
and with each other to develop our ministry. We will
support each other practically and spiritually.

Paying for the ministry

Needless to say, all this technology comes at a price.
Not only will you have to persuade the church that
you need the technology, you are almost certainly
also going to have to persuade them to pay for it.
Milton Baptist Church in Weston-super-Mare had a
unique approach. They began a Technology Fund
and invited contributions. If no contributions were
forthcoming then they would accept that it was
not God's will that the church move into the

multi-media age. But, if funds were forthcoming, they would move forward. Not only were the funds forthcoming, they came in abundance.

Once you have decided what your aims are, develop a plan as to how you will achieve them. You will need to draw up a budget. If the church needs to purchase items, you need to cost it out in full. Don't forget that as well as the big items, such as computers and projectors, there will be the smaller but just as important items, such as extra wires, discs, spare lamps for the projector, etc. Never skimp on this part. Reveal the full cost right at the start. Always buy the best you can afford. Accept, and make sure the church understands, that today's most powerful computer will be outdated next week. Always think about how you can upgrade the facilities you have without throwing everything out and having to start from scratch, remembering that there is virtually no second-hand value in some of the technology you will require.

Think too about installation costs. Will you require professional installation? Will any changes need to be made to the fabric of the building? Will desk or table space be required for the extra equipment? Your answers to these questions could have cost implications. As an estimate, professional installation could add as much as a third to the total cost.

The hardest part may be converting the church to the need for multi-media. According to Barry Whitlow, founder of EternityWorks.com, a Christian entertainment company:

The question is not 'Will the people in your church be open to you using multi-media?' They will. They validate multi-media as a communication medium every time they turn on a television, go to a movie, watch a video, or surf the Web. The real question is how do you start using multi-media in your church? Once you begin, people will become comfortable with its use very quickly.
(Quoted in ChristianityToday.com/Church Buyers Guide – Lighting and Video, 'A Vision for Video'.)

You might need to educate the congregation to look at things in new ways. You might need to educate the minister! Bill Hybels, senior Pastor at Willow Creek, admits that there needs to be balance between the artistic and pastoral teams. Speaking to the Willow Creek Arts Conference in June 2001 he admitted as the only non-artist in an auditorium full of artists, to feeling like 'a Hyundai in a parking lot of BMWs'. He recognised the tensions that can exist between the pastor and the creatives. On the one hand you have the pastor who is trained and filled with theological facts, whilst on the other you have the creative who is used to being creative and emotive. Whilst the pastor wants to be clear about the message, the artist is looking for subtlety, mystery and moving people emotionally. The challenge is to combine the artistic and the theological with integrity. This can only happen, asserts Bill Hybels, when the pastor is prepared to relinquish his ultimate authority, when the artist drops all prima dona style behaviour, and the two teams build a relationship of trust, recognising each others' differences and talents.

All involved are looking for the same result – well prepared, technically well presented services that will enable people to worship. There needs to be good communication between the teams if the service is to work. If what is produced is technically very creative but bears no relationship to the message of the day, then the value of the presentation is lost. Both sides need to work together.

What you do will be under scrutiny. If the technology fails, if things do not go quite according to plan, questions will be asked. What you do is going to be very visible. The need for rehearsals is essential. Don't try to be overly ambitious from the beginning. Start slowly and build up. Allow the church to become used to the technology gradually. Discuss what people like about it and what they dislike about it.

CASE STUDY: Minister and creatives in harmony

Old Roan Baptist Church, Aintree, England

Old Roan Baptist Church began life as a church plant in the village of Aintree, home to the world-famous Grand National horse race. Over the last few years, the church, which meets in a school in the village, has seen tremendous growth. The church's minister John Kearns has been to Willow

Creek Community Church on several occasions. Whilst Old Roan, with an active congregation of around 100 people can not hope to match the resources of Willow Creek, John has applied the same principles to the church.

Sermon series are planned months in advance and John sets himself the task of preparing his sermons in full several weeks ahead of their delivery time. This enables the worship leaders to study the context and the content and prepare their material accordingly. The audio-visual material is also prepared in advance. Despite the smallness of the church and the lack of permanent facilities, Old Roan makes full use of modern technology as an aid to the main message. John's dream is that eventually Old Roan will have its own full-time audio-visual 'minister'.

CASE STUDY: Converting your church

Guiseley Baptist Church, Yorkshire, England

Simon Hammond, minister at Guiseley Baptist Church in Yorkshire recalls that the church has always used whatever it could find to enhance both its worship and its teaching. 'I'm sure,' he says, 'in the olden days they had a flannel graph. When I came to GBC we had an overhead projector. This was used not only for the words of new songs but also for sermon illustrations. Even with the overhead projector, we tried to be as creative as possible, using multi-layered sheets to create dynamic presentations.'

However, the birth of the new set-up at the church really began on a Sunday evening in the late summer of 1998. Simon was preaching to his congregation. From his viewpoint he could see straight down the aisle of the church, out through the glass doors at the front, to where a number of youngsters were congregating. Here he thought was a group of young people who needed to hear about Jesus. The big question was how could he ever get them to come inside the doors of the church? At that moment, he stopped the service and the congregation talked and prayed together about what might attract these young people into the church.

The building at Guiseley had already required a considerable amount of work but gradually it was taking shape. With only a small congregation Simon knew many were already giving sacrificially to cope with the new building work. But, from that evening's and subsequent discussions, the church decided to equip the church with technology that would enable them to present the gospel in a twentieth-century format.

The pews had already gone making way for chairs that could be moved into any formation, or even taken away altogether. The church then set about adding a lighting rig in the church and a projector, fixed on the far wall. With video projection capabilities, computer software and lighting installed – it was time to invite in the youngsters. And, they came. Rock Solid, the church's youth club for the 11 to 14-year-olds grew very quickly and has thrived, subsequently splitting into two groups.

The church is now able to lay on all sorts of events including discos and concerts for youngsters in the town. But, it's not only the youngsters who benefit. Simon regularly uses video and PowerPoint® material during the services. Church meetings are enlivened with photographs and graphics. Simon has learned by experience not to rely entirely on the technology having once been badly bitten during a joint service! However, he does note that when used sensitively, the right picture, graphic, song or video clip can be very dramatic. On the Sunday after 11 September 2001 and the tragedy in New York he used just one image – that of a girl involved in the protest at the school in Northern Ireland. His point? Evil begins when we teach our children to hate.

Getting kitted out

So, to the kit you require:
There are several items that are essential:

O projector and screen (although the latter may not be necessary)
O computer
O presentation software
O video player and monitor(s)
O cabling
O insurance.

Projectors

Video projectors have developed enormously over the last few years. The large unwieldy objects that required three lenses to be lined up correctly are a thing of the past. Today's projector is small, light-weight, and much brighter. They also handle computer-generated text without the need for any kind of conversion facility. As this is probably going to be your most expensive purchase, take your time over the decision about what to buy.

Before purchasing a projector you need to consider a number of things:

O How large is your church, or hall where it is to be used? How bright is the space? Do you have large windows that allow light to flood in?

O Where will you place the projector? Will you be able to suspend it from the ceiling? If so, how easily will you be able to get access to it to maintain it? Can it be wall mounted? If it is to be wall mounted at the back of the church what is the length of the throw to the projector screen?

O Is it possible to back project (that is, have the projector behind the screen and therefore out of sight of the congregation)? Is there sufficient space behind the screen to place the projector out of sight?

O Will you need a screen to project on to? Or, is there a large blank wall? (However, you might want to bear in mind that some screens actually enhance the brightness of the projected image.)

O Do you want the projector and screen to be a permanent fixture?

O What shape is your sanctuary? Will one projector and one screen be sufficient?

O Will you be using the projector to play videos primarily? Or will it be used to display graphics? Or, is it to be a mixture of both?

The answers to the questions above will give you some idea of the size of projector you will require. Light from projectors is measured in ANSI lumens (ANSI is the American National Standards Institute brightness test). The projector has to be able to cope with any light, even ambient light, that is thrown on to the screen. Most churches probably use a projector that has around 1100–1500 lumens and find this to be sufficient. However, it might not be sufficient for your church, particularly if you have any extra lighting facility. Then your projector will have to cope with stage lights as well. Or, great care must be taken to see that stage lighting is directed away from the screen.

The larger churches in the United States, including Willow Creek, use projectors that generate around 5000–7000 lumens. At the Assembly we use projectors that generate 7000 lumens and take four strong men (and I'm not being sexist here, I keep out of the way, they are seriously heavy!) to lift them.

You can also buy smaller projectors (almost literally small enough to fit in your pocket) that generate around 700 lumens. These do not however produce a particularly large image. The size of the final image produced will also have a bearing, particularly if your church has a large building. My advice is to test projectors out. Invite a salesperson to bring some along for you to try. Test it out in broad daylight, preferably when the sun is shining. Don't just look at how bright the image is, check out the contrast and the colours as well. Try using different font sizes for your text. Sit in every area of the church and remember that whilst you might have 20/20 vision not everybody else will have.

Projectors have a fan inside that runs to keep the bulb cool. Be aware of how much noise the fan makes. If you are able to wall or ceiling mount the projector the sound may be less evident. However, if your projector is not going to be a permanent fixture and you place it near the front of the church, the fan may become a distraction, when it is in use, to those seated nearest to it.

When considering projectors look also at whether they are able to reverse the image (essential if you are planning to back project) and whether they have a keystoning facility. The latter will be required if for any reason you are not able to mount the projector or the screen so that both are facing each other exactly square on and on the same level. You may have noticed if you already use an OHP that unless the screen and the projector are exactly square on, the final image projected onto the screen sometimes appears to be larger at the top tapering away towards the bottom. The keystoning facility will allow you to correct this on the projector. The alternative is to angle the screen to compensate.

Remember, if you back project, the final image will be reversed on the screen. Most projectors, however, have a switch that allows you to reverse the projected image so that those seated in front of the screen will see the final image the correct way around.

Check how many video and computer inputs the projector allows. Most now come with two of each. Is this going to be sufficient for your purposes?

Check out the cost of replacement bulbs. Whilst the bulbs have a long life they are expensive to replace. It is worth keeping a spare just in case your projector bulb goes at an inopportune moment. (Let's face it, when do they ever go at an opportune moment?) Look for a projector that has a bulb life of at least 2000 hours. Also, ensure that you do not have to call out an engineer to change the bulb.

Ensure that the projector has a remote control that allows you to switch between the inputs directly without having to cycle through all the inputs, and that you can 'blank', or AV mute, the screen from the remote. Most modern projectors have the latter facility which means you can make changes on your computer without them appearing on the big screen and without having to shut down the projector first. It is best to avoid actually having to shut down/restart the projector too often as this can shorten the bulb life. Also, it takes a few moments for the projector to completely shut down as the fan will continue to run for a few moments to cool the bulb.

'Blanking' the screen allows you to switch from computer to video signals to the projector. Most projectors will always be projecting something. If they are not receiving a computer signal or a video signal they will project either a 'blue' screen, and/or a 'message screen' where words such as 'no signal detected on RGB1' appear. This needs to be avoided as such screens can be distracting in the middle of worship. In order to achieve the most seamless appearance you need to be able to blank the screen as one presentation ends, switch the projector to the next required input whilst the screen is blank, begin the next presentation and 'unblank' the screen.

The next step up from this is to acquire a switching or mixing facility that will allow you to mix between the inputs without ever needing to blank the screen. However, this involves more expensive equipment and is the next step along. Don't worry about it for now. Get the basics first. A suitable remote control and dexterity with your fingers will allow you to keep things moving along without the screen being blank for too long.

Some projector sales representatives may try to confuse you with talk of SVGA and XGA. This is to do with the resolution that you operate your PC at. It is likely that you operate your computer at SVGA which is 800 x 600. (If you are not sure, go to the Start Menu on your computer and scroll to Settings. Select 'Control Panel' – then choose 'Display'. Once in 'Display' choose 'Settings' which will show you the Display Properties of your computer.)

Computers and video signals operate at a different screen resolution. Although today's projectors are billed as video and data projectors, in reality they have to convert the video signal before projection. You can purchase projectors that are XGA (1024 x 768 resolution). However, video resolution is around 720 x 576 and therefore there will be some adjustment and processing of a video image. This may cause some loss of quality in your video image.

Finally, on projectors, buy a reputable brand with a warranty.

Screens

The shape of your sanctuary will have a bearing on the final decision on your screen. Is one screen going to be sufficient? Where will you place it? A single central screen is the most common. If your sanctuary is rectangular, greater in depth than width, the single screen approach can work well.

But some churches prefer to have a screen to one side, particularly if the lectern is central. If this is the case, let us suppose that you place your screen to the right of the lectern as we face the front. Then those sitting in the congregation on the left will look past the speaker to the screen, those who are sitting to the right side will look away from the speaker to the screen. Ask anybody who is used to speaking from the front what it is like to look out at a row of blank faces – then ask them what it is like to look at a row of blank faces that are looking away from them! Your pastor may prefer to have the screen behind him/her so at least people are looking in the right direction.

The further back the screen is placed the greater the angle of view. If the screen is too far forward those seated at the ends of the first few rows may have difficulty in seeing text on the screen in particular.

The height of the screen is important too. Is there sufficient ceiling height in the room to allow the screen to be above the pastor's head? What will the angle of view be for those in the front row? I'm all for looking up to sing, but I prefer not to be expected to do an impression of an astronaut during lift-off in order to read the words.

It may be that the shape of your building militates against even entertaining the idea of back projection. However, if it is a possibility consider it seriously. The noise of the projector fan is immediately reduced. The projector itself is out of sight. Be careful that the projector is at a sufficient height to the screen and that there is no light spill under the screen from the lamp.

If you are planning to back project, check out whether there is any loss of brightness. Some people maintain that you can lose around 25% of the brightness of the image when back projecting. (You'll notice that I don't particularly subscribe to this view: I think it depends on the equipment – but check it out with the equipment you plan to use.)

You could be very scientific about the placement of the screen and draw a scale plan of your sanctuary and the seating and work out the angle of view. My less scientific suggestion is that you test out the screen in situ. If you have yet to purchase a projector or screen use an overhead projector and screen as substitutes for testing purposes.

You can of course use an ordinary OHP screen to project on to. This will not allow you to back project. Most OHP screens come on tripod legs and will move given the slightest opportunity (a small breeze, somebody walking by, etc). Decent projector screens are stretched on a frame and are sturdier. If you intend to move between locations and may want on some occasions to front project and on others to back project you can purchase one frame and two screens. The screens are then affixed to the frame via press-studs. You can also make your own screen. Guiseley Baptist Church (see case study) have a permanent screen made of 12 × 8 ft (3.5 × 2.5 m) of awning canvas stretched on a lightweight wooden frame. (Note the word 'stretched'. Unless you are going for a particular effect the screen needs to be taut on the frame.) Proper screen material can be purchased on a roll if you plan to undertake a DIY job.

It may be the case that a screen is unnecessary. Milton Baptist Church in Weston-super-Mare rebuilt its church a few years ago. The design allowed for a large white wall behind the lectern on to which all the images are projected. Milton have thereby avoided one of my 'pet hates' – the blank screen!

Most screens in use by churches are around 8 × 6 ft (2.5 × 1.8 m). If they are a front projection screen they are matt white, if a rear projection screen they are a dull grey, and there is no disguising them; they are very obviously there. In some churches the screen is used only for projecting the words to the hymns and songs. This means that for around probably 75% of the service they sit there ... blank. More about this later.

Computers

I'm not going to tell you what to buy! The decision as to whether you require a permanent computer, dedicated specifically to the task, or whether you use a laptop will depend on a number of factors.

If you are designing presentations a permanent computer fixed in the sanctuary presumably necessitates you having another computer elsewhere on which to work. The two need to be of a similar specification. Preparing a fast-moving graphic presentation on your home computer that slows to a crawl on the church computer will be very disappointing. The advantage of a laptop is that at the end of a service you can unplug it and walk away.

If you work on the laptop to produce presentations there is no problem about having two sets of software. You also avoid the possibility of walking out the front door one Sunday morning, leaving behind your discs with all your carefully prepared presentations which require loading on to the church computer.

If you are loading material from discs (whether they are floppies or CDs) always copy the material to the hard drive or desktop of the machine you are running the presentation on. Your presentations will run faster.

Depending on the software you choose (see later chapters) you may well require two graphics cards and/or two screens.

A DVD player on your computer will give you access to high quality (in the technical sense of the word) films. Make sure you have the right cable(s) to take sound from your computer to the PA system. A CD writer will allow you to save the best of your presentations in library form, perhaps for later use or use by another church. You can also create backup discs of regularly used material.

So, once again, choose the best computer you can buy. Make sure it is upgradeable – can you add more graphics cards, more memory, more hard drive space should you require it?

Jean Smith runs the presentations at Milton Baptist Church. Jean custom-built the computer that they use in the church. The specification is as follows:

750 MHz AMD processor, 256 MB SD-RAM, 30 GB hard drive, 52-speed CD-ROM, Dual header Matrox Millennium 32 MB graphics card, 56K modem, 17-inch monitor.

According to Jean, this specification has 'been perfect for the past year or so and we're not looking to upgrade just yet'. I offer this to you as a guide only. Bear in mind, that what is up-to-date today – will be out-of-date tomorrow. In the time it takes you to read this book, computers will have been upgraded, changed, improved ... Windows XP® will have become something else...

Video Players

It is worth spending a bit extra on a video player and buying one that has a jog shuttle facility. This will allow you to line up exactly to the moment that you wish to start playing from. If you are going to show videos regularly it is also worth investing in a monitor (small TV) that you can check the video on before you hit the play button to the main screen.

Video projectors are good for projecting the image from a video player but not so good for replaying sound, particularly in a large room. You will need to feed the video sound through your PA system. This may have a bearing on where you place all your kit.

Cabling

You will need to think about your cable runs. If you decide on rear projection, you will require a cable run to wherever the operator sits. Even if the operator sits behind the screen, think about the video sound. It is most likely that your sound desk/PA system is controlled from the rear of the church. You will either need to have a long cable run between the video projector and the video player – assuming that the player is near the sound desk, or a long run between the video player and the sound desk if the player is also with the projector and computer. There is something to be said for front projection where the projector is as near to the back of the church as possible and the sound desk, video player and computer are all in one place.

My own personally preferred option is keep all the techies as close together as possible so that everything can be co-ordinated. (Unless you really want to get technical and start using headsets as a way of communicating between the techies.)

An obvious point, really, but do be wary of your cable runs. Gaffer tape is a wonderful invention – you can stick it down on floors and carpets to hold cables in place and pull it up again afterwards without any damage to floors, carpets or cables. Although, don't be too complacent, like any sticky tape it has a tendency to tie you up in knots if you are not careful with it! If you can possibly design your layout so that cables go across the ceiling and down the walls then do so. The ideal, of course, would be to have all your cables behind the walls.

Software

This deserves a whole chapter to itself. So, in the next chapter we will look at the different software available and how to use it.

Insurance

Very obvious really – but do ensure that all this lovely new equipment is insured. Lightweight, portable projectors are easy to drop! You might want also to think about some basic rules as to who is allowed to use the equipment. Organising rudimentary training courses and only allowing those who have been on the course the use of the equipment is no bad thing. If you are relying on the technology on Sunday and somebody drops the projector on Wednesday ...

Do's and don'ts

So, to recap, here's a list of do's and don'ts in respect of equipment:

DO buy the best you can afford.

DO try before you buy.

DO buy a computer that you can upgrade if necessary.

DO ensure that all your cables are securely taped down – there's shouldn't be a single loose strand of flex across any floor!

DO make sure you insure all the equipment.

DON'T rely on the video projector for your sound output.

DON'T let just anyone play with the equipment.

CHAPTER 3

Making the Presentation

This will be the starting point for most churches. The decision is taken to move on from either using hymn/chorus books or an overhead projector and to use presentation software on a computer projected on to the big screen or wall.

I would like to make it clear that I don't believe the OHP has entirely had its day. At times, the portable OHP with some well-produced slides, can still prove particularly useful, especially if you are presenting a talk in a small church to a small group of people and you don't want to have to worry about setting up a projector and computer. However, how many times have you sat in services whilst somebody at the front puts the typed sheet of words on to the OHP upside down, or too far to the right and the ends of the words have disappeared? Or, worse still, the slides have been produced in landscape format only to find the OHP to be in portrait format. If you are at all concerned about the professionalism of the presentation you can't beat the computer/projector partnership!

Presentation software

I'm assuming that you are using a PC, although there is very little difference if you do happen to be Mac-based (although Mac users tend to think that they are better off than PC users!). The choice of software is plentiful but it is most likely that you will be using Microsoft's PowerPoint® for the simple reason that many computers you buy 'off the shelf' come pre-loaded with Microsoft Office, which often includes PowerPoint®. So we will begin our consideration of the software with this most widely used product. If you happen to have a version of PowerPoint® earlier than '97 I suggest you upgrade immediately. The earlier versions were more limited and for the purpose of this book I am referring to the later versions.

It is possible that you have already used PowerPoint® for presentations at work or at school/college. If so you will be familiar with its possibilities and its limitations. You will also be aware that many people will have seen it in use. It is no longer the 'surprise package' with which to 'wow' people. Many people will be familiar with the templates that come supplied with PowerPoint®, they may have seen it in the latest business presentation they attended, or, perhaps even used it themselves. At church on a Sunday we want to create something a little different, something that will take them away from the world in which they are living and working. With a little creativity and imagination it is possible to use PowerPoint® to produce some imaginative results.

If you have never used PowerPoint® before and need some training you will find that local colleges run evening classes – six to eight weeks on the use of PowerPoint®. Personally, I wonder what takes so long! My suggestion is that you open up the software and play with it.

But, if you really do find it helpful to have some teaching, you can visit `www.ebibleteacher.com/tipsprep.html` for a website that teaches PowerPoint®. Or, visit `www.zdeducation.com`. This latter company provides CD-ROMs that allow you to 'learn at your own pace'. You can also order the discs through `www.office-associates.co.uk`.

PowerPoint® works as a system of blank slides on which you can select background colours, type your text and add animation for effect. These animations allow anything you have placed on the slide to be introduced in different ways as you run your slide show. You can also change the way that the slides follow each other – the transitions.

You can insert graphics, photographs, sounds, even movie clips. But remember the more you add to each presentation the larger the ultimate file will be and not every computer will have sufficient memory to be able to run the presentation in the best manner. However, to keep your presentations to a reasonable size it is worth noting that photographic images need only be scanned at a low resolution (72 dpi is fine) for use within PowerPoint® presentations.

Eventually you will become bored with the standard background colours offered by PowerPoint®. At this stage you need to begin experimenting with the background template. There are several options. You can go to www·presentationpro·com and buy a selection of new templates. Presen-tationpro.com also offers a design service for creating your own custom designs. www·churchmedia·net is an online resources store which also sells backgrounds for PowerPoint®.

You can of course create your own. You may want to design a template that is relevant to your church. You can use your own images as a background slide. To do this you will need to scan your own images (unless they are taken with a digital camera) and save them in an appropriate file. Open up PowerPoint® and choose 'Blank Presentation'. Then choose the appropriate slide (I tend almost always to use the blank 'auto layout'). Then select 'Format' and 'Background'. In the box that opens click on the 'Background Menu' drop-down menu and click on 'Fill Effects'. From the 'Fill Effects Menu' click on the 'Picture' tab and then click on the 'Select Picture' box. You can now browse your files to find your appropriately saved picture and click on 'OK'. You can then choose to apply this as your background picture on just one slide or on all. Remember of course, when choosing pictures, if you want to use text over the picture you will need to choose both your picture and text colour with care if you want people to be able to read the text.

The more you play with the software, the more you will discover what you can do. In this chapter I have inserted some examples of different types of slides to show what can be done.

Once you begin to feel very creative you might want to consider investing in additional software such as Adobe Photoshop™ which will allow you to create all kinds of images and backgrounds.

Hymns/songs

Let's start with your most likely use of PowerPoint® – hymns/songs. There are a few do's and don'ts:

DO choose strong colours for your background and your text. For example, strong yellow works well on a blue background. (Note: this is actually my personal preference. Some churches prefer to go for a pale background with strong colours for the font. This would not be my preference. But, you must decide for yourself. Do not mix colours that are close together in the colour spectrum, e.g. yellow/green; blue/red; blue/green. Consult with dyslexic and colour-blind members of the congregation for possible problems to avoid.)

DO use a point size for your font of at least 36 and bold. (You can get away with a 32-point font size but generally 36 is best.)

DO use a font that is easy to read. This is not the time for experimenting with fancy text. My personal preference is for Arial. (Times Roman is too fussy and narrow with a very slanted italic form.)

DO use the same font throughout.

DO make sure there are no spelling mistakes.

DON'T overfill each slide with text. As a rough guide you should only fill the top two-thirds of the slide with text. This will depend upon the height of your screen. But remember if your screen is fairly low, when people stand up to sing, those sitting at the back of the church may find the lower part of the screen obscured by heads.

DON'T use ALL CAPITAL LETTERS – it actually decreases readability.

DON'T use the feature of lines flying in from left and right.

DON'T use custom animations on the slides – the words should just be there.

DON'T use the random transitions to move from slide to slide, in fact don't use any transitions at all!

DON'T allow spelling mistakes ... yes this is in here twice! It is important to check carefully what has been typed. An event I attended in America was due to finish with a liturgy. It should have been a moving moment, bringing together the last four days of worship. Instead, there were so many dreadful spelling mistakes that the audience for the most part were convulsed with laughter. The moment was ruined.

Unless you have all the hymns/songs already on computer somewhere, you (or somebody) are going to have to complete the task of typing in the songs. There are various suppliers of song software on discs. If you have a CCLI licence, which you must have if you intend to reproduce hymn/song lyrics (see later chapter on copyright), you can have access, for an additional fee, to SongSelect®. This software gives you over 3000 hymns/choruses in a format that can be cut and pasted into any Windows-based software. It will still require some time and patience to get the songs into a suitable format for PowerPoint®.

If you use these, make sure that the song version is the version that your church uses. It is amazing how many slightly different versions there are of the same song! Do check also with your worship leader for any slight alterations that they may use, such as singing the chorus as an introduction, or repeats of the chorus.

Each song should have its own separate file. Save the song with its full title and be particularly wary of those that have similar, or even the same, titles. It is always worth adding a blank slide at the end of a song. During the service it is easy to get carried away and press the mouse key again at the end of the song by mistake. This will bring up the 'slide sorter' view on the big screen – something to be avoided at all costs. The congregation should never see the 'nuts and bolts', only the end result! For this reason, I never use the right click on the mouse when the slide show is in progress. This brings up a menu that allows you to perform a number of tasks, including forwarding the presentation. I have seen people using the right click in order to go forwards or backwards through the presentation whilst running it – again, I think this is allowing people to see the 'nuts and bolts'.

If you are working with PowerPoint® '97 you will need to have a print-out of your slides. PowerPoint® allows you to print out up to six slides to a page. Make a note of each slide number. If the worship leader goes back through the chorus in a different order you can jump from slide to slide by using the numeric key pad on the right of your keyboard. (You can use the numeric keys and enter pad on the main part of the keyboard and on a laptop this will be your option – but using the numeric key pad on the right is simpler from a speed of use point of view.)

If you are using PowerPoint® 2000 and have two video cards and dual monitors you can keep the song list on one monitor whilst displaying what is going to the projector on the other monitor.

When it comes to the service, make sure you know which hymns/songs are to be used and either ensure you have all the files opened on your machine, or you may prefer to create one file with every presentation to run through on the Sunday.

It is possible to jump between presentations that you have opened during the service without blanking the projector. You need to open your presentations and using the 'Alt' and 'Tab' keys you can cycle between those that are open. However, you do need to be fairly quick as a small dialogue box does open up in the centre of the screen and you also need to be sure which presentation you need to move to. Anything that might distract the congregation is to be avoided. So, I would suggest, that unless you have

incredible dexterity and memory recall you blank
the projector screen whilst switching between
presentations.

Other presentations

Once you, and the church, are comfortable with the
use of PowerPoint® for the hymns/songs it is time to
move on and begin experimenting further. Think
about how else you might want to use the technology.

Notices

These can be made into a presentation that runs
before the service. The presentation can be set to run
automatically in a loop. This is your opportunity to
be a little more adventurous with the presentation.
Photographs, animations, different transitions – this
is the moment. But, don't overdo it! Some of the congregation will be preparing themselves for worship,
so don't shock them too much. Thornton Avenue
Baptist Church in Fremont, California, makes a
feature of the notices during the service. Before the
pastor comes to speak, the lights are dimmed and
the notices are run on the big screen accompanied
by some suitable music.

Bible reading

The reading is projected on to the big screen. Make
sure the text is large enough to be readable (at least

36 point font size remember) and without any distracting background. (Some may object to this as an idea arguing that it discourages people from bringing their Bibles. But there will always be some people that don't bring a Bible and unless your church supplies them ...)

Sermon notes

Simple bullet points, headings, Biblical references. Don't over do it. The notes are there to complement the sermon not take over from it. They must not be too distracting. The congregation should be concentrating on the pastor not the screen!

Background images

This is where your imagination and creativity comes in. Presentations can be used in a variety of different ways. Here's just some ideas:

○ I was in a church where the youth pastor sang a song to the young people during a service marking the end of their Summer Camp. It was a powerful song, well sung, about the choices they would face in the future. The screen behind remained blank. What a shame – it could have shown images of the young people, making it an even more personal moment for them.
○ Reports of events, such as the Summer Camp mentioned above, can be accompanied by images.

○ Information on coming events, such as a Church Weekend Away, might have photographs of the proposed venue, simple information on dates and costs.

○ For the more adventurous, well-prepared images to accompany music soundtracks that have a message.

Basic rules for presentation

An organisation called RUN (Reaching the Unchurched Network) supplies to members a CD with a number of PowerPoint® presentations pre-loaded. These are copyright free to members. If you are into technology, RUN is an extremely useful organisation to be aware of. You can visit their website at www.run.org.uk. They also offer training in PowerPoint® as well as news and information on the latest resources. Further contact details for RUN can be found in the address list at the back of this book. The presentations include rules for presentations.

There are a few rudimentary rules for using PowerPoint® (or whichever software you choose).

First thing to remember is that the screen is there to complement the message. Don't try to overfill the screen with words. Giving the congregation too much to read serves as a distraction from the main speaker.

If you are using bullet points to complement the speaker's address then those bullet points need to come in as the person is saying them. This is not an exact science and you really need to do it almost by instinct. Let me give you an example. My boss was giving a presentation on the book of Romans. The slide is headed 'The Heart of the Gospel (Romans 3:21–26)'. There are then four bullet points:

○ In the law court – the guilty are acquitted.
○ In the slave market – the slaves are set free.
○ In the temple – the sacrifice is accepted.
○ Justification/redemption/atonement.

Now, as he says the first line 'in the law court – the guilty are acquitted', I would bring in that line as he reaches the second half of the sentence. By the time the line appears, and people are able to read it, he has finished the sentence. It reinforces the message without revealing the 'punch line' too soon.

As I say, it is not an exact science and you will probably want to practice getting it right. It helps if you are operating the graphics for somebody whose style of delivery you know well.

It is of course quite possible for self-operation. Some projectors allow you to load the disc directly into the projector and run the presentation. Or, you can use the infrared remote operation of your computer. The remote control device that comes with your projector can be linked to the infrared remote port on your computer. To do this go to the Start Panel on your screen, click on Settings – Control

Panel – Infrared – Options and then click the 'Enable Infrared Communication'. Then, by pressing the forward button on the remote control your computer will automatically forward the presentation. This means you can place the computer and projector further back in the room and you have no need to be physically next to it whilst giving your presentation.

Personally, I prefer the operation to be separate from the speaker. Having spoken many times using a laptop and projector I am aware that it is a distraction having to forward your presentation. If somebody is handling it for you it allows you the freedom to move around, be more natural and to relax – after all, there is one less thing for you to think about.

Finally, and I can't stress this enough, prepare with your presentation! Or, if it is somebody else's presentation, make sure you have looked through it. Be sure you know which slides build and how they build. Is each animation operated through a mouse click, or does it happen automatically to a set time? I prefer always to have a print-out of the presentation so that I can follow it through and mark up any notes for myself on the printed version.

The professionalism with which you run the presentation will have an effect on the speaker and the congregation. The speaker, because they will be able to concentrate on their delivery. The congregation, because you won't be distracting them, but will be aiding them to concentrate.

Some do's and don'ts for presentations

DO rehearse the presentation.

DO have a print-out of the material.

DO run presentations from the hard drive of your computer, not from a disc (floppy or CD).

DON'T let your presentation distract the audience from the speaker.

CASE STUDY: Using PowerPoint® creatively in a church setting

South Oxford Baptist Church, Oxford, England

The Revd Simon Carver, minister at South Oxford Baptist Church, decided to experiment with Powerpoint during church services. He turned the church sanctuary into a café and developed a number of different presentations to explore various themes. One theme was on the way we change and develop as we grow older. Using his own life as the main theme he used photographs of himself through the years alongside strong images representing the different decades. Another presentation was developed on the way we look at God. Using people images set against a stark black background, Simon asked questions using white text against the same stark black background, such as 'If God had a face, what would it look like'.

The presentations showed how the medium can be used much more creatively than many of us might ever have imagined.

Example customised slides

The slides on the next two pages are examples of
different PowerPoint® presentations:

Figure 3.1 is a Baptist Assembly 'Opening' slide –
this slide involved scanning some specially commis-
sioned artwork by artist Eddie Askew on the theme of
'Disciples at Dawn'. Scans were taken from different
areas of the paintings supplied. These were then used
as background templates for various slides used during the Assembly. For some of the slides the intensity
of the artwork was reduced using Adobe Photoshop™.

Figure 3.2 is a basic song layout using an existing
PowerPoint® background.

Figure 3.3 shows the background of another of
Eddie Askew's paintings used as a notice slide at
the 2001 Assembly.

Other presentation software

Whilst PowerPoint® is the most widely used software,
other presentation software is available on the market.
You might want to look around at some of the other
options. Some of the software now available has been
written specifically for use within a church setting.
Most of it is American – but then so is PowerPoint®!

Before you make a final decision you need to ask
yourself some questions:

○ What are we going to be using the software for?
○ Is a song resource all we need?

THE
BAPTIST
ASSEMBLY
2001

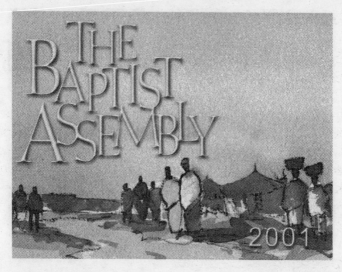

Figure 3.1

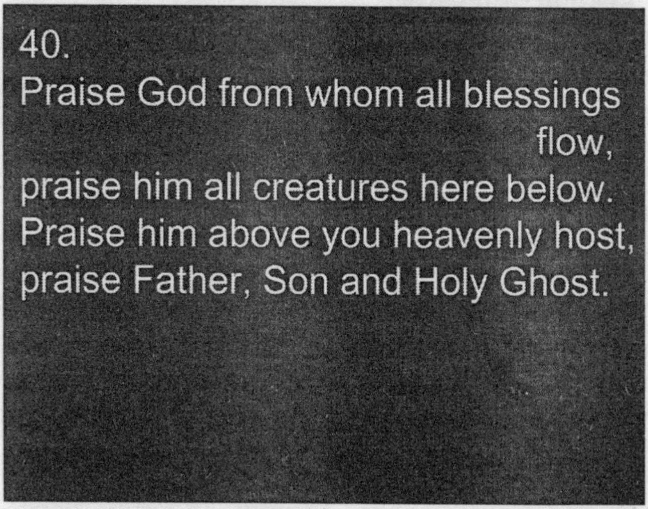

40.
Praise God from whom all blessings flow,
praise him all creatures here below.
Praise him above you heavenly host,
praise Father, Son and Holy Ghost.

Figure 3.2

This morning's offering is for
The BWA

Figure 3.3

- Will we be developing presentations that are graphic-intensive?
- How easy to use does it need to be? How many different users might require training?
- What extra features does it offer, if any?
- Will we need to upgrade our computer to be able to use it?

To run most presentation software you are going to need at least Windows 98, 64 MB of RAM, two graphics cards and sufficient hard drive space.

Corel Presentation®

Not too dissimilar to PowerPoint®. Some of its animations and transitions are slightly smoother. You can import PowerPoint® material into Corel Presentation®.

Prologue Worship Leader

A dual-screen application which therefore requires two video cards. PWL works on a 'bin' format. You store your images in different bins and assemble your final presentation by opening the required bin and dragging the required element into a cue list. Like PowerPoint®, backgrounds can be solid colours or images imported from the image bin. It is possible to display the entire song, allowing you to choose different parts at random.

Prologue Sunday Plus

This appears to be a newer version of the above. It has many features including the ability to fade between separate slide files, to make amendments to slides even when you are running that particular file, to insert sudden announcements into a file as you are running it (useful if you need to ask a parent to attend to a child in the crèche), and some very attractive screen wipes. Visit `www.prologue.cc` for a look at this software.

Presentation Manager

Another dual-screen application. This software includes something like 3000 songs – if you have a CCLI licence (see section on copyright issues for information on CCLI). Five Bible translations are also included. This enables you to project songs, Bible passages and presentations. An extra feature allows you to overlay words on to live video. There is a search feature which allows you to quickly look up songs and/or Bible passages. Visit `www.cre-ativelifestyles.com` for a look at this software.

Other presentation software

This is only a sample of what is available and you could spend a long time examining all the different software available. However, some advice – decide what it is you need. Visit some of the sites of software manufacturers who often offer a download of a trial version. Try some out. Be wary of buying the latest, all-singing, all-dancing software from a company that you have never heard of. If they go out of business you could be stuck with some software that nobody else knows how to use, is not upgradeable and will need to be replaced.

As you become more adventurous with your presentation software you will begin to discover its limitations. You will want to put better images as backgrounds. Inevitably you will want other software that will allow you to manipulate images, such as Adobe Photoshop® or PaintShop Pro®.

You may want to use more of your own photographs. So, do you take your photographs with an ordinary SLR and scan in the finished product? Will you require a scanner? Or, will you invest in a digital camera and import images directly into your computer? It is worth investing in a good quality digital camera. The final images can be superb. They tend to be capable of taking good quality images even in a low light situation. The ability to take as many photographs as you like, perhaps deleting the odd 'duff' one as you go, and to check to see instantly if you have achieved a result is an extra selling point.

A good camera will allow you to take images at different resolutions. It is best to take and store the photographs at the highest resolution possible and then reduce the resolution when importing them into your presentation.

Using sound as part of your presentation

This is the part where I sound like an old fogey! Music can often provide a great backdrop to a presentation. Let's assume you want to use the latest big-selling pop song in your presentation. You and I might be able to hear the words. We might be able to sing them by heart! But, there will be many people who will neither know the song, nor be able to understand a word of what is being sung. If your presentation relies upon people being able to hear the words of the backing track you are using, you are probably going to need to incorporate the important words into your presentation.

CHAPTER 4

Using Video

There are likely to be two uses for video in your church. Firstly, you will be playing back pre-recorded videos (whether your own or other peoples' work) and secondly, you might want to use cameras for reasons we will discuss later.

If you are using graphics, (i.e. running PowerPoint®) and want to add video to your system you will need to have some way of switching between the two. At the most basic level you can switch between the two on the projector. Most projectors will come with a remote control so when you want to change the input you can use the remote. You will need to ensure that you have a clear line of sight between you and the projector to enable the infrared remote to work.

Pre-recorded videos

But let's look first at the use of the pre-recorded video. All pre-recorded videos, movies, DVDs, material you have recorded from the television – it is all copyright material. The law is the law. If you want to show a clip from a movie you need to obtain permission, or have the appropriate licence (see next chapter on copyright issues).

There are other sources for material that you may want to explore using in church. Willow Creek produces a number of videos, particularly of their drama sketches.

Before you show any video you need to ask yourself what the purpose in showing the video is? Is it to illustrate a point? Is it to educate the congregation? If so, it needs to fit in with the rest of the service. Is it an advertisement for an organisation? Trinity Church outside of Chicago was sending two of their congregation out to work with the Mercy Ships organisation. The couple were moving to another state to work in the head office. Before the couple came forward to the front of the church for prayer and commissioning, a short video was shown that illustrated the work of the Mercy Ships organisation. It was an effective use of the video. But that same video may not have worked so effectively if it had been shown out of context during a service. Then it might have been more appropriate to show it in a home group where it could be discussed.

There are dangers inherent in showing film clips as one organisation found out during a conference. A speaker chose to show a clip from the film *The Shawshank Redemption*, a powerful film about a man wrongly imprisoned for the murder of his wife. In the film, Andy, played by Tim Robbins, is a banker and is able to get alongside the warden by keeping his accounts and advising him on the stock market. During this process Andy also negotiates with the authorities for a library for the prisoners. During the clip shown Andy is seen receiving boxes of books and records in the warden's office. Left on his own he locks all the doors, flips some switches and plays part of an opera over the loud speaker system to all parts of the prison. The inmates are spellbound. In voice-over we hear the sound of his friend, an older and wiser prisoner played by Morgan Freeman, explaining what that music meant to the prisoners.

That point should have marked the end of the film clip. The picture was dropped but unfortunately the sound wasn't faded out quite fast enough. The entire audience heard quite distinctly, Morgan Freeman's explanation, in slightly 'colourful' language that the warden was less than happy about it!

To an audience of artists and technicians it was an amusing moment, perfectly understandable, after all, we've all probably been there and done that! But, in your average Sunday service the congregation might not have been quite so appreciative.

So, beware, if you plan to show a film clip and you have any concerns make sure that everybody knows the 'in' and the 'out' cues to the second!

Shooting your own

It may be that you have shot your own 'home' video. Old Roan Baptist Church in Aintree had compiled footage from various different services. They have turned this into a ten-minute video on the life of the church which is given out to newcomers.

Of course, shooting your own home movie is not quite that simple. Somewhere along the line you are going to need to edit the material. These days there are software packages that will allow you to do this. Adobe Premiere® is one that we use. This works like the much more expensive systems available to the professionals in that you select the shots you require from your material and digitise them onto the machine. You are then able to select the final images, moving them around, trying them in a different order, adding effects, etc. Editing video is however memory intensive (not yours, but the computers!). You will need to have plenty of gigabytes of hard drive available.

Video sound can also be a problem. If you are shooting something which requires the audience to be able to hear what is said your original sound must be of the best quality. This will almost certainly require you to invest in additional sound kit. Whilst the fixed microphone on most domestic camcorders is adequate for general noise, it will not be adequate for picking up clearly the spoken word.

Today's audience is generally assumed to be more sophisticated when it comes to television watching. Apparently we expect the highest quality production values. But, actually that's not entirely true. We are also used to watching documentaries that are shot on lower quality formats. There are all kinds of programmes these days that are shot mostly on the industry standard, Beta SP, but have inserts that are shot on DVCam or DVPro. Most people would probably be hard pressed to identify the difference. So, don't be concerned about getting out and about with your camera. Besides, we all love to see ourselves on television. There are those touching moments when proud Mums and Dads turn up with their camcorder to record the children participatin – baptisms, weddings, special services – the quality may not be of television standard, but they still have meaning for us.

There are other ways in which you might want to consider using video. If you've travelled on an airline recently, you might have seen as you near your destination, a video that shows the layout of the airport that you will be arriving in with a brief explanation of where to go to collect luggage, catch buses, taxis, etc. This same kind of video could be shown before your service. A brief explanation of what is on offer, where to take the children out to Sunday School, perhaps even what happens during the service. It can all be part of making the visitor feel more at home. If a video is too complex, then the above could be produced as a PowerPoint® presentation.

Using cameras in the service

Some churches are already making use of cameras to relay what is happening on the stage onto the big screen. The cost of large broadcast standard cameras may be prohibitive but many churches get by with smaller domestic camcorder cameras.

There are a number of reasons for using cameras within a service, both to replay the images and also videotaping:

○ image magnification – quite simply, making it easier for people at the back to see
○ allows people to feel, and to be, more involved
○ provides a different perspective
○ allows those not able to be in the main sanctuary to be a part of what is going on
○ recording the service for shut-ins or missionary partners overseas
○ local television, cable or terrestrial, output
○ a record of special services and/or events
○ for streaming on the Internet.

At Willow Creek, in an auditorium seating around 5000 people, Bill Hybels still likes to use a flip chart to illustrate the points he is making. In such a large auditorium this might seem like a strange thing to do. After all, only the first few rows are going to see what it is he is drawing. But, because they use cameras to magnify the image, everybody can see Bill's drawings. He can still use the preaching/teaching style with which he feels comfortable – the technology will ensure that everybody can participate.

The kit required

As ever, when buying technology there are lots of choices to make! First you need to take a look at the different video formats available. You may already have access to video cameras. But, here's a quick run-down of the different tape formats:

○ VHS – what your video recorder at home plays.
○ S-VHS – an improved quality VHS format. S-VHS tapes, whilst looking identical to your VHS tapes, won't actually play on a normal VHS video player.
○ 8 mm – another improvement in format but now outdated.
○ Hi-8 – yes, you've guessed it – the next improvement in 8 mm. Still used (occasionally).
○ Mini-DV the next, next improvement! This is actually of broadcast quality.
○ DVCam – finally, the version that is of broadcast quality.

As you've probably guessed the final two are digital formats – hence the great improvement in quality.

When you choose your camera(s) there are a number of things to look out for:

1. Does the camera have the ability to switch from auto to manual focus? Have you noticed how sometimes when you are using the camera you are aiming at one thing, then somebody walks across your path and the camera readjusts the focus on that nearer object. It's what I call 'hunting'. The camera is hunting for the image to focus on. To avoid this, I prefer to use a camera in manual focus.

2. Does it have a white balance facility? This is essential if you are going to be using more than one camera to relay images on to a screen in your church. Essentially, this allows you to balance the colours correctly in the camera. You switch on the white balance feature and point the camera at something white, perhaps a piece of white card (or all cameras at the same white object). The camera then automatically adjusts its colour balance.

3. An 'In' socket for an external microphone.

4. You might want to consider looking for a camera that can change its image size ratio from 4 x 3 to 16 x 9. For those of you with a widescreen television you will know that the latter is widescreen size.

5. Can the camera be switched on and left on without being in record mode? Many modern camcorders automatically switch themselves off after a while if they are not being used. If you are using them to relay a service you will obviously require the camera to remain switched on, but not necessarily recording, for some period of time. (Keep in mind that some cameras will stay on if there is no tape in the camera.)

6. Is it possible to use a different lens on the camera? What is the zoom of the present lens? Might you want to use a wider lens for a different angle?

7. All cameras should have a lens cap – sounds obvious, I know. But this small, but vital piece of equipment is what protects your lens – make

sure it's the first thing that gets used once the camera is switched off.

There is another vital piece of equipment – the **tripod**. You might just look at it as the object on which you rest your camera, but a good tripod is invaluable. Make sure that your tripods are sturdy and sufficient for the weight of the camera and that they will withstand the occasional knock. Some lightweight tripods will tremble if the floor shakes a little. Let's say your camera is close to the drummer, when he or she goes into full rock drummer mode, the floor will shake a little. Make sure your tripod won't.

Check that you can pan (turn side to side) and tilt (move up and down) smoothly with the camera fixed on to the tripod. Does the tripod have a quick release plate which enables you to lift the camera off the tripod in a hurry? Some more expensive tripods come with a spirit level built in. This allows you to check that you have the tripod straight and level. You could, of course, buy a small spirit level and carry it with you in your little 'gadget' bag that will also include lens cleaner, spare video tapes, and other useful items you discover that you can not live without.

Training

If you are planning to relay the video image from the camera(s) onto the big screen, then do make sure your camera operators are trained. One thing viewers are used to seeing is well-controlled camera work. There are a few simple rules for camera work:

1. Make sure the shot is in focus!
2. Never perform a pan followed by a zoom either in or out. The two actions should be performed **together**. As you pan (turn the camera from left to right, or right to left) perform the zoom at the same time. This requires some practise to achieve successfully, but the end result is much neater and will look more professional. In the same way, never perform a tilt followed by a zoom.
3. Practice with the tripod for smooth pans and tilts.
4. Try not to use too much camera movement. Cameras that are constantly on the move, panning, tilting, or zooming, are likely to send the congregation home feeling distinctly seasick.
5. When composing shots, leave a little 'head room' (i.e. room above the person's head), unless you are in an extreme close-up when it is okay to lose just the top of the head (but not the mouth).
6. Leave room in the shot for movement. If you know your speaker has a tendency to walk around, then keep the shot wider (but not too wide) and leave room for him/her to walk into the space in the shot.

Learn the technical terms for the shot you require:

○ Wide shot (WS) – as it sounds, an all-encompass-
  ing shot with the camera on its widest angle lens.
○ Mid shot (MS) – the person in the frame from the
  waist up .
○ Close-up (CU) – the person's head and shoulders.
○ Extreme close-up (ECU) – the person's head,
  losing the top part of their head and possibly
  part of the chin but not the mouth.

If you want actual camera movement, invest in a
tripod dolly (a set of wheels for your tripod) and make
sure that the floor is smooth. You can try doing clever
hand-held shots but only when you are really experi-
enced at moving the camera smoothly around.
Generally in order to do this you need to cradle the
camera in your arms, holding it down around waist
height, rather than trying to hold it on your shoulder.
The latter is true, particularly if you are using a domestic camcorder without any kind of shoulder pad. I'm
constantly amazed when I watch people walk around
with domestic camcorders held at their eye level. Arm
ache sets in very quickly and the movements become
jerky. Most cameras have a moveable eyepiece, or even
a screen that tilts. This allows you to turn the eyepiece
upwards and, cradling the camera in your arms, move
around in far greater comfort.

Multiple camera operation

If you are going to introduce cameras into the service you need to make some decisions. Are you

going to have just the one camera or more? If more than one, how will you mix between the cameras? How will the camera operator know when his/her camera is 'live'?

Multiple camera operations are complex and require more (and expensive) equipment. If you plan to use cameras to relay the service then it is best to start with just the one.

If you do plan to use more than one camera, you will also require a switcher or a vision mixer (preferably the latter which allows you to cross-fade between pictures and add effects), preview monitors and a final output monitor. The preview monitors allow the person operating the vision mixer to see the shot that each camera operator is providing and to select which shot to use at any one moment in the final mix.

If you are using a mixer, you can also take the graphic and feed the output through the mixer. This would allow you to mix between your graphics and any video material/camera shots. If you choose to do this, you will require a scan converter to convert your graphic image to a video image.

Figure 4.1 (p62) shows the basic set-up used for the Churches Together in Britain and Ireland Assembly. We did not have the resources to use cameras at this conference but I have added these in to show how they would have fitted into the con-figuration if we had.

Figure 4.2 (p62) illustrates the technical set-up for the Baptist Assembly when we used just one screen (or three screens utilising the same image).

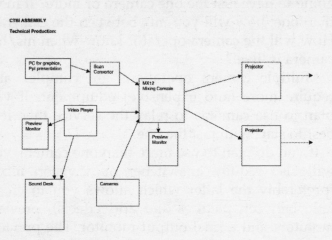

Figure 4.1

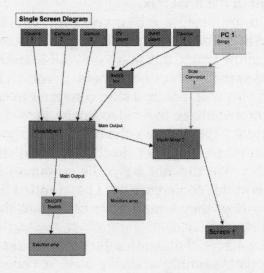

Figure 4.2

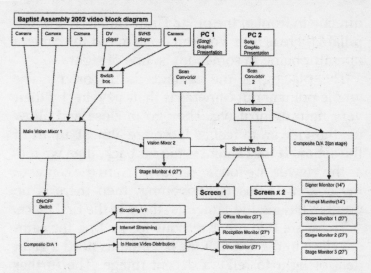

Figure 4.3

Figure 4.3 gives the technical set-up for the Baptist Assembly for a three-screen set-up, where the output is divided between the main screen showing one image and two further screens showing a different image.

At Milton Baptist Church, Weston-super-Mare, believers' baptisms are now always videoed using three cameras and a vision mixer. The actual baptism is also projected onto the wall so that people at the back can see what's happening. Looking to the future, the church is planning to buy special unobtrusive cameras to answer recent complaints about the camera rigs/camera operators being distractions. This will always be a problem in buildings that are not purpose-built. If you have pillars you may be able to place a camera operator with rig directly in front of the pillar. Unfortunately, without pillars there is little you can do to avoid the camera operator being in somebody's 'line of sight'.

The placing of the cameras is important. The whole point about cameras is that they are, by their very nature, intrusive. They go in close and allow us, the viewer, to feel as if we are almost a part of the action. If the camera is too far back, then we too, as the viewer, are too far removed from the centre of the action. If this is happening, then there is no point in having the camera(s) there in the first place.

There are two other reasons for getting the camera close to the action. One is, cameras need a great deal of light to relay a decent image. The further distance the camera is from the image, the greater the light required on the image to get a decent shot. Secondly, if the camera operator is having to rely on full zoom to get in close to the action there is more likelihood of the final shot being in what I politely term as 'wobble vision', that is the image will be more prone to shaking. Please don't rely on those wonderful devices on your domestic camcorder that are meant to eliminate 'wobble vision'. Remember that your final image is going to appear on a large screen with the slightest imperfections magnified for all to see.

If you are using more than one camera, place them carefully. Do any of the other cameras appear in another camera shot? If you are shooting action on the stage and the screen is directly at the back of the stage, it is easy to end up with the multi-layered approach on the screen. You end up with a shot, within a shot, within a shot. Personally, I like this effect – at certain times! But it is not such a great shot if you are filming one person speaking and suddenly they appear in multiple on the screen behind.

If you are using multiple cameras and they are feeding to a vision mixer you will be running many more cables around the building. Also, if you plan to have one camera roving about as a hand-held, this should become a two-person operation. One person to hold the camera, one to make sure the cable never gets wrapped around the camera operators legs or anybody else's! (This latter person is known as a 'cable basher'.)

So, before you get into the multiple camera arrangement think carefully about placement. There is also the argument, put forward by Dennis Choy at North Coast Community Church (see Case Study, below) that having a single camera shot in a fixed position allows the audience to feel a part of what is going on, particularly when that audience is in another room. I have always been an advocate of the multi-camera shoot. However, I sat at North Coast Community Church and watched the main address being relayed into the video café. Because the shot never changed, I was faced with the preacher speaking directly out front, for 40 minutes. At one point, he began to move slightly out of shot and the camera had to move with him. At that moment the spell was broken and I realised I was involved in a televisual experience. Until that point, I felt I was part of a normal Sunday congregation!

Being filmed can also be difficult for the pastor. Trying to maintain eye contact with anyone beyond the first few rows is impossible as most are looking past the pastor to the screen(s) behind. It also takes some discipline on the part of the pastor. At one church I visited, I found myself operating their remote control cameras from the 'gallery' when the remote control camera operator failed to turn up. In this particular church they use seven cameras, three remote controlled, to record the service for broadcast the following Sunday. The pastor preaching that Sunday (who was not the senior pastor of the church) would look off to the left of the church and be picked up on the camera there. He would look to the right and be picked up on the camera there. But for some reason he would not look directly ahead at the camera facing. In the 'gallery' we were 'willing' him to look at the central camera because in the final mix it looks as if he is completely ignoring the central blocks of the church.

Your church may well have a crèche and in many churches the sound is relayed to those taking care of the children in the hope that they may be able to hear what is going on – if the children give them a chance! The next step is to use a camera and relay the service on a monitor to them. A single camera shot is perfectly acceptable for this. In the same way also, cameras can be used to relay services to overflow facilities. Perhaps your church gets particularly full at Christmas, Easter and/or special services.

Cameras can also provide new ways of 'doing' church. Whilst some churches are using cameras to enhance their services, others are using it to provide multiple worship services.

CASE STUDY: Using video to provide satellite services

North Coast Community Church, Vista, California

North Coast Community Church is just 21 years old. Originally started as a house group meeting it has grown to a membership of several thousand. As the church grew it bought a building on what we would call an industrial park. The unit comprised the main sanctuary, which seats around 700, the church offices and meeting rooms. It wasn't long before the church was too large for the main sanctuary and extra services were added.

The church began to meet on Saturday evening and twice on a Sunday morning. But, still the numbers were too large for the capacity. It was agreed that, rather than add another service, the church would experiment with a satellite service and they took another unit nearby. Chris Mavity, one of the staff, felt that people should not be punished by having to be in the overflow. It was important that the overflow unit be an experience for those attending. This led to the Video Café.

Worshippers in the Video Café would have their own worship band, their own worship leader, but join with the main sanctuary in seeing the message via a big-screen video link. As compensation for getting the message via a video link, worshippers also had the option of drinking coffee and eating doughnuts and pastries. The Video Café soon became a great success.

As the church continued to grow so North Coast added more satellite services. The worship in the Video Café is more acoustic in nature; Traditions offers traditional worship; The Edge is for those who like their music electronic and loud.

Dennis Choy is responsible for the audio-visual services at North Coast. He points out that there are two important aspects of the services they offer. Firstly, all worshippers regardless of which satellite service they attend experience the same message. This forty-minute teaching session is also then carried through in mid-week growth groups. It helps to maintain the cohesiveness of the congregation. Secondly, they use only a single camera in the main sanctuary, in a fixed location to film the main speaker. The camera rarely needs to be moved. This helps those watching in the satellite areas to feel that they are truly participating in the message – it avoids it becoming a merely 'televisual' experience. 'The only people who ever ask me why I don't use more than one camera are production people,' laughs Dennis. 'Everybody else just gets involved in the message.'

Whilst the congregation might believe that on Sunday they are joining with the main congregation, in fact they receive a video taped version of Saturday night. The cabling for both video and audio has a substantial distance to travel and therein lies the potential for technical difficulties. 'Next time,' says Dennis, 'we will use fibre optic cables and it will be better.' The present video tape system requires Dennis to watch through the video message whilst copying it for each of the venues to ensure that there is no 'drop out' on the tape. 'Most people can cope with a glitch in the visual but if the audio drops out they tend to be more concerned. Consistency of sound is all-important.'

North Coast's satellite services require a large number of volunteers to run the technical side. Each venue has a sound engineer and a PowerPoint®/ video operator. For most services a third person acts as a producer, gently reminding the engineer and operator when things should happen. 'It's easy for someone who is busy with PowerPoint® to forget that they need to lower the stage lights as they begin to run the video. The producer is somebody who can see the whole picture,' explains Dennis.

As North Coast continues to grow so it is looking for new premises. But plans to build a larger sanctuary have been scaled back. 'We are looking for one that will hold around 1200 people and we will continue to offer the smaller satellite venues. We can then keep that intimacy in worship, even though the church is growing so fast.'

Video as an aid to worshipping God

Once you start to use the technology you will find all kinds of uses for it. But remember, it is a steep learning curve for everybody! The creative possibilities for your presentations are endless and as with so many things, once you start experimenting, you will want to go on to discover new and even more creative ways of working. Remember though, your presentations, for the most part, are only there as an aid to worship. They should not get in the way of allowing people to draw close to God.

Before we finish this chapter, a brief discussion on my 'pet hate' – the blank screen. If you use a video camera and also some kind of presentation software it is possible that you can fill the screen with an image of some kind for the whole service. This will take some planning. But you could have a graphic image with your church's logo on it, or the text for the day, or the text for the year. This could become the 'filler' screen in between hymns/songs or video camera relayed shots. Again, it doesn't have to be anything too fancy, or distracting.

Some do's and don'ts for using video

DO check that you know the 'in' and the 'out' point on any video/DVD clip and ensure that both sound and vision operators know it too.

DO check videos for quality control.

DO ensure that the cameras you purchase are adequate for the task.

DO make sure you train your camera operators.

DON'T rely on flimsy tripods.
DON'T rely on 'camera sound' if you are shooting
  your own videos.

What to do when it all goes wrong

If there is one thing you can guarantee with technology, it is that it will let you down. Computers
will crash on you, or at least your operating software will give up and usually when you least want
it to happen. Videos will suddenly have a glitch.
The sound will fail. A bulb will blow in the lights.

One Sunday, I was attending a church where they
were using a laptop running PowerPoint® and a
projector to project the words to the hymns/songs
on to the wall of the church. The very full congregation was singing heartily as was the pastor,
despite having his back to the screen. Suddenly I
noticed a battery warning light appear in the
middle of the screen. The operator, discovering that
his laptop wasn't properly plugged in to the power
decided to push the plug in hard. The computer, for
reasons known only to itself, took exception to this
and decided to quit. Suddenly, only the minister
was still singing heartily, completely oblivious to
the fact that the congregation was now staring
bemusedly at the sight of the computer throwing a
wobbly. As the operator rushed to restore the
screen, he didn't bother to blank the projector. So,
the congregation was treated to the start-up process
of the computer Windows graphics.

Eventually the minister realised that the congregation was no longer singing and that he was now performing a solo. He turned around to see what was happening on the screen behind him and the problem was revealed. Fortunately, being an extrovert helped in this case and he recovered the situation with expertise.

Two things to note here. One is operator panic must be avoided and secondly having a monitor on the stage so that whoever is leading the service can see what is going on is helpful. The second is slightly more technically challenging, as it will entail more cabling. The first is down to you!

Preparing the way for the occasional technical glitch is wise. Always have a 'Plan B'! Make sure that anybody involved in leading the services, and therefore likely to be at the front when things go wrong, are well briefed. Prepare the congregation also. Their reaction to a technical hitch can be crucial. Let them know early on when you are introducing the technology that things might go wrong.

When the computer does crash, the first rule is 'don't panic'! The next thing to do is 'blank' the projector screen. Inevitably it will take a while for you to re-start the computer and however long it takes, it will feel twice as long. But, if the service leader is well briefed they will be able to move swiftly to a song that perhaps everybody knows without needing the words – and, hopefully the worship band will know it too. Or, they could move to a time of prayer.

If your video clip is vital make sure that the person using it is aware of the content. If his or her talk depends upon it they will presumably know it fairly well and may need to resort to the old method of describing the clip and allow people to imagine it!

Some pre-arranged hand signals between the operators and service leader are valuable. That way you can let them know if this is a temporary, permanent or perhaps fatal error!

CHAPTER 5

Copyright Issues

The issue of copyright is complex so I thought it best to give it a chapter of its own. In the United States of America a licence is required to show clips from feature films. Willow Creek Community Church plays many such clips throughout the year and on each occasion they will find out who the distributor is, contact them for permission, and obtain a 'Public Showing' licence on payment of the correct fee. Once they have the licence they can go to their nearest Blockbuster and hire the film. There are some distributors who apparently always refuse to issue a licence and included in this is the distributor of the *Star Wars* series of films. In Britain the position appears to be different and somewhat confusing. Having pursued this with the copyright licensing agencies in this country and spoken with other organisations who use video and music clips in presentations, the picture is still unclear! Different people seem to have been given different advice. Let me suggest that if you are in any doubt you contact the Copyright

Licensing Agencies direct (see Appendix for useful addresses).

Let's suppose that you do want to use music in your presentations, show videos or DVDs or just play a pre-recorded music track. We can't continue to ignore the copyright issue, so the first thing to note is that all music is copyright and you can't play it without permission or a licence.

How you plan to use music, video, DVDs, etc will determine the action you need to take. Trying to obtain permission to use particular music, say for a video you might have made, can be a very hit and miss affair. Some large churches/Christian organisations make contact with record companies and beg for permission to use a particular piece of music. Sometimes the company agrees and sometimes it doesn't. As a film student, a fellow student and I made a documentary about gorillas and used 90 seconds of music by the rock musician Peter Gabriel. As an internal college project that was just about okay. However, the then TVS factual department decided to show the documentary on television. Various negotiations took place, but it still cost around £6,000 to pay for the 90 seconds of music. I was just glad that TVS were footing the bill!

There are music libraries that produce CDs of music in an enormous range of styles. The CDs themselves are free, you pay for the use of a particular piece of music. How much you pay depends upon how you intend to use the music. For instance, if you are producing an advertisement, or a video, which utilises library music, you will pay

more than you will for a one-off use in a presentation. The people to contact are the Mechanical
Copyright Protection Society (MCPS) who will send
you a sheet of forms for your use. These are to be
filled in and returned with the details of the CD you
use, what you used the music for, and how much
music you actually used. MCPS for their part
ensure that you are on the mailing list of various
music libraries who will send you material at peri-
odic intervals. You could also contact the libraries
yourself and ask for CDs of music in a particular
style.

It is most likely that you will be reproducing
hymns and/or worship songs for projection; making your own arrangements of existing music
pieces; and playing pre-recorded music and film
material.

The first people you need to turn to are **Christian
Copyright Licensing International** (CCLI). CCLI
originally began by concentrating on copyright
clearance for the reproduction of hymns and worship songs. But, as churches have begun to use
other copyright material, so CCLI has developed,
branding itself as a 'one-stop shop' for churches
and their copyright issues.

CCLI produce a useful leaflet that sets out the
various licences required. With regard to the reproduction of your worship material you will require a
CCLI licence. This covers you for the reproduction
of hymns and worship songs on overhead projector
transparencies, computer projections and on song-
sheets.

At present, if you are using pre-recorded music within the context of a worship service, no licence is required. However, if you use pre-recorded music on the church premises for other events, perhaps as part of entertainment, you will need a **Performing Rights Society Church Licence** (PRS) and a **Phonographic Performance Licence** (PPL). These are available from PRS and PPL. Slightly confusingly, CCLI are agents to PRS but not PPL. You might think it strange that you require two licences to play pre-recorded music. This is because there are two copyrights involved. The PRS licence is granted on behalf of music composers and their publishers. A PPL licence is granted on behalf of record companies and recording artists.

What about feature films? The best advice I could get from PRS was that a church holding a PRS licence could show whatever they liked providing it is in the context of worship and within the church's main worship area as a PRS licence covers you for the use of any public performance of copyright material. So, we are in the strange situation of British churches presumably being perfectly at liberty to show clips from any *Star Wars* film it chooses, whilst in America, home of the *Star Wars* movies, no such opportunity exists! However, there are a few things to note. You are not allowed to do anything that will infringe the copyright in the work. So, you are not allowed to re-edit movies to suit your own purposes. (Well, imagine if you are James Cameron and you've spent several years working on your masterpiece, *Titanic*, and somebody else comes along and re-edits your work in a form that they prefer – would you be happy?) Any clips must be shown from an original copy and without any other embellishments, such as an accompanying drama or different music.

A PRS licence is available through CCLI as agents to PRS.

If you are not showing a film/video as part of a worship service and you do not have a PRS licence you might like to know about a company called Filmbank Distributors Ltd. This company hires out and licenses films for both private and public showings. Films can be hired for around £60 plus VAT for the first day with the charge reducing to £30 plus VAT per day for subsequent days. The audience can be up to 250 people and you can show the whole film or part(s) thereof. Once again, if you show clips you must not tamper with the original footage in any way. Filmbank provide the copy of the film and you will need to rewind or fast forward to the appropriate places as they will only provide one copy.

CHAPTER 6

Sound and Lighting

Sound

However good your graphic presentations, or your videos, if people are not able to hear correctly then the value is lost. One probably fairly obvious point, but I'll say it anyway, there will be people in the congregation who are not yet ready to use a hearing aid and make use of the hearing induction loop that is probably a part of your sound system, but for whom hearing is becoming a problem. When hearing starts to go, the first thing lost is the ability to distinguish particular sounds. Cranking up the volume that bit extra does not actually help much. The clarity of any sound is the most important thing.

It is important to determine if your existing PA system is adequate for quality transmission of music or whether it was designed mainly for amplifying speech. You may have a sound system which is adequate for mixing and recording purposes but lacks good quality speakers. The distribution of sound in the auditorium also requires expert advice regarding position, direction and number of speakers.

A brief word on auditorium acoustics might be helpful. The acoustic properties of churches, halls and theatres vary considerably. This is because some surfaces reflect sound while others absorb sound. It is well known that good acoustics prevail in large stone-built churches and buildings with plain plastered walls where sound reflections produce a resonance and presence that is pleasing to the ear. However, some modern buildings are designed – by intent or default – to absorb sound which creates a flat response to the listener, either with music or speech and especially during congregational singing. This is usually caused by such features as wall-to-wall carpeting, large curtains, rough-cast brickwork and particularly absorbent ceiling tiles. (Church architects sometimes specify sound-absorbent tiling in the mistaken belief that religious buildings should be designed to muffle voices as in a library.) Plain reflective surfaces are a great benefit to creating the best acoustical atmosphere for worship and stage performances.

It is worth noting of course that when the building is full you will need to turn up the volume – people's clothing absorbs sound very well. So, remember, once you have performed your sound check in any empty building, be ready to turn that volume control up a little further once the building is full.

There are plenty of very technical books written about sound. It is likely that your church will already have a sound system and a competent sound engineer(s) to run it. Your main concern will be ensuring that any sound from your presentations/videos is run correctly through the system, with correct cues given for the start and finish of an item.

This is where you will really appreciate the importance of working as part of a team.

Lighting

Perhaps you are producing seeker services with different elements, maybe some drama, some video, music and you want to use some lighting to draw attention to the different elements. At the most basic level you may just want to be able to lower the level of light in order to show a video.

There are plenty of technical books written about lighting. Unless you already have a lighting rig in your church, you may be in the dark (no pun intended, honestly!) about lighting.

Two well-recommended books are:

○ *Stage Lighting Step-by-Step* by Graham Walters, A&C Black
○ *The Stage Lighting Handbook* by Francis Reid, A&C Black

Read them in the order I've recommended them. The former has many colour photographs to illustrate how lighting works, the latter is more text based but goes into greater detail.

So, why is lighting important? Lighting can be used to great effect in many areas – you don't need to wait to put on a full-scale theatrical production to use lights. Simple drama sketches might require some lighting. You might want to add more light to the lectern. Look above church pulpits (in those that still have them). How often is there a light above? That wasn't there only to give the preacher light to read by – that often came from a lectern light – but to illuminate the preacher, to draw your attention to the preacher and to benefit from facial communication and body language. That is what light does – it reveals things to us. Anybody can turn all the lights on, but we need to learn how to be more selective. How we use the light can determine what we draw attention to and receive information from.

If you are recording the service on video, although most camcorders can cope with fairly low light levels, for a reasonable final image you will need to scale up the brightness on the stage.

Before you make any decisions about lighting, read up on the subject. Draw a scale plan of your building and decide what it is you require. Too few of the wrong type of lights can create a disappointing effect. Too many of the wrong type of lights can do likewise. Ask yourself what results you are likely to require. Is it a blanket colour wash of the stage and/or the backdrop? Are you likely to want spots at any time? If you can really only afford a few lights then make sure you choose the right light in the right position.

A light that is too high, shining down at too acute an angle will not be flattering to your subject. Shadows will appear around the eyes, nose and chin. Light that is too low will give the subject a scary look! Ideally the main light source needs to be in front at an angle of around 30-40 degrees to the subject.

There are a number of different types of theatre light (or 'lanterns). The two most useful to a church for a basic lighting plan (see below) are fresnels (pronounced frenel) and profiles. Fresnels are used above and to the side of a stage and are the lights that provide general lighting as they are capable of giving a softer, diffused light. They are focusable and can also be used with attachments called 'barn doors' that allow you to shape the light, or prevent it spilling over into areas that you do not want to light. They can also be used with colour filters to provide a colour wash. Profiles are used in front of the stage and provide the front lighting for people. They ensure that we can see all the detail of a person's face which is important for communicating the message and retaining audience attention – facial expressions are an essential part of the message. You are not able to use barn doors or colour filters on a profile although they can be fitted with (expensive) colour changers or scrollers. You can also use 'gobos' which are heat-resistant metal discs with various shapes cut out of them. By placing these in the lantern different effects can be created. You can buy gobos with a variety of shapes cut out of them, or you can have a gobo cut to your own design.

In previous years at the Baptist Assembly we had our logo painted on to the stage set, or cut out of polystyrene blocks. However, since we discovered gobos, we have found out just how much more versatile our logos can become – now, we can project them onto walls, or the ceiling or the stage set, bringing them in and out as we wish. The only drawback is, once your gobo is in the light that light is no use for anything else. You will need to set aside a light for this specific purpose.

Here's a basic lighting plan:

○ If you can only afford ONE light – it needs to be at an axis off the horizon 30–40 degrees up straight ahead.

○ If you can afford TWO lights – then they need to be 30–40 degrees up and around 60 degrees apart

○ If you can afford THREE lights – add a backlight to the two above – this will move the person forward from the background.

○ If you can afford FOUR lights – add a light on to the background to give stage depth.

○ If you can afford EIGHT lights, double the above, placing the second set seven to eight feet away, along the stage.

○ If you can afford TWELVE lights, place the next set a further seven to eight feet away along the stage.

And so on....

The above is a very basic lighting scheme. You really need to read up on the subject and decide what is right for your church.

At the same time you should also investigate the benefits of uplighting and indirect lighting for the creation of non-glare daylight illumination in the auditorium which does not detract from viewing the rostrum area.

Of course, lights have to be operated from a lighting console. Today's digital lighting systems allow you to pre-programme lights and run them from a computer-based system. But, look out for the manually-operated boards with faders because they may be going cheap somewhere and could well be perfectly adequate for your purposes.

Remember that lights have to be fixed somewhere. If you are going to be hanging lights above the congregation they must be properly secured. If they are on stands, then the stands must be properly secured. Again, make sure all your cables are secured with gaffer tape.

Remember also that the lighting is there to draw attention to what is happening on the stage. It is not there to draw attention to itself. Occasionally you will want to use it for dramatic effect. But, don't overdo it! Lights that chase around all over the place, flashing on and off are fine for rock concerts but they don't have too much place in a worship service. At the Blackpool Assembly we finished the Sunday evening Communion Service with a version of Handel's *Messiah*. The *Messiah* was on video, with the words coming up through moving patterns on to the video screens. As the video played, and the sound pumped out of the speakers, we used the lighting on the flats replicating the patterns on the video screens. It was quite awesome! But, the video and lighting effects were taking place across a 40-foot stage in a huge arena. In a small church, it might have been too much. The other important point to note was the context in which this all took place – a communion service where people had been covenanting together as God's people. Originally, we were planning to play the *Messiah* video as people were leaving the hall at the conclusion of the service. But, there was such a strong sense of God's presence and a desire to continue to worship that we took an instant decision to drop the houselights and run the lighting and video sequence.

The context is all-important, which is why I am never keen on videos of events – you have to be there to share in the true experience.

Some do's and don'ts for sound and lighting

DO make sure you work as a team.

DO ensure clarity of sound for every presentation, video, etc that you do. If people can't hear it, the moment is lost.

DO ensure that lighting changes match the mood of the moment.

DON'T allow your lighting to spill on to the screen.

DON'T use effects just for the sake of it.

CHAPTER 7

The Church on the Internet

This is a subject that could easily fill a book, or two ... and has done. So, I'll try to avoid getting into all the arguments about whether you can use the Web to evangelise and try and stick to the fundamentals of how your church can use the technology of the Web as part of your worship.

There are many churches that are now using their website to broadcast their services, either in audio or in audio and video. Within the UK the former appears to be the most popular whilst in America many of the larger churches are broadcasting their services in both sound and vision. For American churches, many of whom will have been broadcasting their services on local television channels and community stations, the use of the Web is merely the next logical step. Within the UK the Web has provided churches, previously denied the right to do so, the opportunity to broadcast freely.

But, before you get carried away and rush to broadcast, let's ask some basic questions about your church website.

The church website

Before you begin building your website there are
seven questions that you should ask yourself (prepared by the American Baptist Churches' National
Ministries Office of Information Services):

1. Whom are we trying to reach? Who is the target
   audience?
2. What will be the source of the content for our
   church's site?
3. Who will maintain the site, and how often will
   the material be refreshed?
4. How might we measure the impact of our site?
   By e-mail responses, requests for more information, increased attendance, decisions for Christ?
5. How will we promote the site after it is developed?
6. How will we follow up on contacts from our
   website? Who in the church will be responsible
   for responding to e-mail, form queries, or telephone inquiries?
7. What time and money resources are available for
   the church's Web efforts?

The likelihood is that your website will be serving
two audiences. Firstly your own congregation who
might like to check out who is preaching on Sunday,
what the Youth Group are up to, collect the sermon
notes from Sunday, and just be reassured that their
church has a presence on the World Wide Web. The
second audience will be those visiting or perhaps

new to the area and looking for a church to attend. They may be established Christians, they may be new converts, or they may just be enquirers. Perhaps they are looking to get married in the area. Calvary Church in Los Gatos, California, handles the two audiences well (although not perfectly) on its website's Home Page. The page is divided into two main sections. The first gives the times of the services and the kind of service it will be. A link immediately underneath takes you to directions to the church. (Unfortunately, if you are not sure where Los Gatos is in California, this site does not help you!) The second section on the page provides two further links to information on the person and work of Jesus and some basic life questions.

The next question you need to ask in relation to your website: what is the most important information that people need to have?

If I am looking up a church on the Web it is probable that I am planning a visit. Therefore, I need to know:

○ Where the church is.
○ What time the services are.
○ Where I can park.

How often have you looked at a church website only to find plenty of information about the ministry of the church but you have to go several pages in before you find out these essential facts? These key facts ought to be on the Home Page, the page that most visitors will come to first. Regular attenders will know all this information and can skip past this page to the information they require. You can expect them to work a little harder for the information. But, not your first-time visitors. You need them to be able to find basic information immediately. Have your full address including your postcode on the Home Page. Websites such as www.Mapquest.com allow you to plan routes by entering your own postcode and that of your final destination. As a visitor to your church, I can type in my own postcode and your church's postcode and be given detailed directions from Mapquest as to how to reach you. You might want to point visitors to your site to such a facility. Some church websites have their own directional map, giving the precise location of the church.

Your website should reflect your church. If your church is lively and has plenty of activities then your website should reflect that. If you only have two people in your youth group, don't let your website give the impression that you have a thriving youth work. Some people searching websites may be looking on a 'try before you buy' basis. They want to have a feel for the kind of place their local church is. For those of us used to walking through the doors of a church Sunday by Sunday we may have forgotten just what a daunting prospect it is for some people. The website allows people to remain anonymous until they choose to take the step of walking through the door.

How easy does your website make it for them?

The Web is another example where technical expertise and creativity need to be balanced in harmony. Somebody who is an enthusiastic website developer may not be the most creative person. Good writing skills are essential, as the messages on your website need to be clear and concise (and without typing errors). It also needs to contain accurate and up-to-date information.

Jakob Neilsen's article on 'Writing for the Web' suggests that you should write 50% less for the Web than you would in a written article. Most people don't actually read the text; they scan it. So, unless you are loading on lengthy articles, or sermons, then keep the writing succinct. Use headings, colours and hypertext to draw attention to key points.

Keep the site simple. The more you put on the site, the more you will have to maintain it. If you plan to keep it updated weekly, then update it weekly. But, websites can become all-consuming, devouring your time. So, if realistically, you know that you won't have time to update the pages every week then devise pages that need updating less frequently. If your church has a three-month plan with sermons and speakers lined up in advance then use this as a page on the site.

Whilst thinking about keeping the site simple, think about how long the site takes to load. If you are spoilt and have the latest, fastest computer that downloads images and graphics in the twinkling of an eye, spare a thought for the person trying to access your site from an old machine. Whilst pretty pictures and flashy graphics are fun, if they take too long to load you will lose your visitors quickly.

Do maintain your links. I've lost track of the
number of websites I've visited where the links to
various pages no longer work. Perhaps the link is to
a site that no longer exists or has moved. Either
way, check your links on a regular basis. A 'surfer'
might not stay on your site as long as you would
like if you frustrate or annoy them.

Evangelism on the Web

The jury is still out on this one as far as I'm concerned. When I'm asked if it is possible to 'do' evangelism on the Web my usual response is a very
quick 'no'. Whilst people may well want to turn to
Christian websites to find out information on
Christianity, its central beliefs and tenets, I don't
believe that many people will be looking to their
local church web page to convert them and give
them what they need to enter into a relationship
with Jesus Christ.

Having said that, Harvest Crusade is an evangelistic
ministry in Riverside, California. You can visit their site
at www.harvest.org/. Every week they broadcast,
in both sound and vision, live events on the Web
which are evangelistic in their nature. According to sta-
tistics reported in Christianity Today.com, (June 14,
1999, article by Jody Veenker) around 45 people a week
accept Christ through the site. What is not clear is what
happens to these   people following their acceptance.
Do they join the fellowship, or another local fellowship, or do they remain listening in via the Web?

There are other sites that are aimed at evangelisation over the Web. Gerald Boyd is a retired minister living in California. At the age of 81 he uses the Internet to communicate with non-Christians. He only began using a computer when he was challenged to become an 'Internet missionary'. He purchased the necessary equipment and taught himself how to go 'on-line'. In one year Gerald Boyd was able to lead 50 people to Christ. Here is an example of how the Internet can be used and also how it is not necessarily the domain of the young! His website is `amazinggrace.com` on which he hosts daily chats. (His site is listed by `OnMission.com`.)

Whether or not you feel that your church website is the place for evangelism is a discussion you must have within your church context. We will return to the subject briefly when we look at broadcasting over the Internet.

Building your site

The days when you needed to be able to understand HTML (the language of the Web) in order to build a site are over. Today, anybody with a computer and software such as Microsoft's Front Page or even Word can build a web page. There are software packages on the market that help you design your pages. Before you buy, be sure about what you require.

You may prefer to go to a website designer. This is clearly a more expensive route but it could be worth it in the long run. Remember, for many people, their first introduction to your church could be through your website.

Two essentials for your site will be a hosting company and the registration of your domain name. Obviously the shorter the name and the more obvious the better. If you can include the town name in the address all the better. After all, how many churches are there with the name 'St Mary's' or 'St Mark's'? A helpful site for information on how to register a domain name is `www.webevange-lism.net`.

Once you have your website you need to register with search engines, which will help people find their way to your site. You should register with all the major search engines as well as with any Christian Internet directories. Different search engines work in different ways. You will no doubt have your own list of favourite search engines. Two of my favourites are Askjeeves.co.uk and Dogpile.com (Whilst the latter's name might be a bit suspect, it works well!).

Don't, however, rely on search engines to push people towards your site. As well as registering your name with search engines make sure it appears on literature everywhere you can think of. Your headed paper should carry it, your church notice sheet, your magazine. Do you advertise your services in the local paper? If so, make sure your Web address is on the advertisement. Ask for links to your site from any national or regional church sites (and be prepared to reciprocate). Does your town or community have a website? Ask for links there also.

Resources for website designers can be obtained at:

O www.web-evangelism.com
O www.gospelcom.net/guide/
O www.brigade.org/today.articles/web-
  evangelism.html

To subscribe to a fortnightly web evangelism bulletin, send a blank-email to:

O Web-evangelism-subscribe@lists.
  gospelcom.net

Broadcasting over the Internet

As high-speed Internet connections become more available 'broadcasting' or 'streaming' over the Inter-net is growing in popularity. For a relatively modest investment churches can now reach a world-wide audience.

As ever, there are some questions to ask before you take such a momentous decision:

O To whom are we broadcasting?
O Can we afford to broadcast in both sound and vision?
O How will we let people know what we are doing?
O What are the legal requirements?

The Web is so widely available that it is almost impossible to answer the first question. It may be that your church has a large number of shut-ins who nevertheless have access to the Internet. You may want to make services accessible to them. Perhaps you have sent a number of missionaries abroad – now they can keep up with their 'home' church. But there will be others, those who have never been near your church, who may come across your site by accident and, assuming that you are broadcasting sound only, listen in. So, how will you ensure that the service is still relevant to them, particularly if you are only broadcasting sound? This is another occasion where the pastor and the creative team must work together. The pastor needs to remember during the sermon that there may be people listening in a very different context who can neither see him or her or the situation of the church. Perhaps you might want to consider adding some photographs to your website on the page from which people access the broadcast. A couple of photographs of the church, one exterior, one interior and the speaker for the day would be sufficient.

Holding on to your website visitors

Although we use the term 'broadcasting' to refer to what we send out over the Internet it is more properly referred to as 'streaming'. There is an essential difference between broadcasting over the Internet and broadcasting over the radio and on television. Television and radio (and the print media) push information out. On the Web however we need to pull people in. Visitors must be enticed in to our site and then kept there. Having a website is only the beginning:

○ If you have registered with the various search engines visitors may go direct to your 'broadcast' page. Where would you like them to go then? Is there another page on the site that you would particularly like to direct them to? How will you create a link to that page that they will be keen to follow?

○ How will you deal with somebody listening in who wants to follow up something that they have heard? Will you have an e-mail address for people to respond to? If nothing else, it will be a good way of gauging response to your broadcasts. Who will be responsible for responding to enquiries?

Legal and other limitations

Broadcasting in vision as well as audio will bring its own set of problems. This would assume that you already are using cameras to record/relay your services. Obviously broadcasting pictures as well as words is more complex. The Web technology is still catching up. If you have ever tried to log on to a major event that is being broadcast over the Internet, particularly pop concerts, you may well have discovered just how fragile the Web can be. Its capacity for handling large numbers of 'hits' (visitors) on one site is not infinite. Now, I'm not suggesting that your church is instantly going to be bombarded by a huge number of visitors (perhaps you have higher expectations than I do) but it is worth being aware of the limitations. Broadcasting video will require a larger server streaming and will be a more expensive exercise for you.

Be aware of the legal issues as well. If you are planning to broadcast the whole service there are copyright implications because you will be singing (performing) material that is copyright. You must in any event have a PRS (Performing Rights Society) licence to broadcast your services over the Internet. You must contact PRS and complete the necessary paperwork before you begin broadcasting.

CASE STUDY: Broadcasting on the Internet

Upton Vale Baptist Church, Torquay

Upton Vale Baptist Church had been using the Internet for some time, having had a website for a number of years. In 2000 the church changed to a local cable provider for its telephone provision and the new provider offered a good deal on ISDN lines. Steve Cayley, a church member who works for Devon Education Authority as an IT consultant, suggested that the church should look at the possibility of broadcasting their services over the Internet. The suggestion met with an enthusiastic reception from the minister, deacons and elders and the congregation. The idea that the church should begin broadcasting in both sound and vision was quickly quashed by Steve Cayley who suggested that they should take it one step at a time!

The church use the services of a local ISP (Internet Service Provider), Eclipse Internet, who host a Real Streaming server. The church then ran an audio line from their sound desk to a computer in the church office. Steve notes that the ideal place for the computer would have been alongside the sound desk but using the church computer avoided the need for the purchase of a second machine. The church computer has Real Producer software installed which connects to the Real Server at the ISP using ISDN dial-up. Real Producer and the Real Server negotiate and should maintain a connection. The Upton Vale Baptist Church website has a link which directs users to the relevant file on the server. Steve also notes that using a streaming server means it is capable of supporting a large number of concurrent connections, which is why Upton Vale uses this method.

A licence to broadcast is negotiated with PRS on an annual basis. This has to be included in the final cost, although Steve notes that costs work out at around £5 per week.

The sound mix is all-important. It is fortunate that Upton Vale have excellent facilities in this area and are therefore able to produce a good final mix. In fact, the excellence of the sound quality has often been prominent in the feedback received.

The Web Pages provide a feedback e-mail address and feedback has been received from folk listening all over the world including the Seychelles, Sweden, USA, Canada, Spain (a member moved out to live in Spain and listens). Of course, there are also those at Upton Vale who for whatever reason have been unable to get to church and have listened in at home. The feedback received from them has been very positive. The church is planning a big publicity drive in order to make more people aware of the site.

Steve notes, however, that there are still a number of issues to be resolved. He is conscious that often speakers rely on visual aids, drama, and audience participation – none of which make for good 'radio'. It is hard to remember that there may be another audience out there, many of whom may even be outside of the UK. This raises the key question of 'who is our audience?' 'Are our services suitable for anyone to listen to?' asks Steve. 'It certainly performs a service for our church folk who are away or unable to attend (it is noted that some only connect for the sermon!). Personally,' he says, 'I have my doubts that it is generally suitable for non-Christians unless they are real seekers with some contact with church. So, should we change our services to meet this need or do something different?'

The church is considering the possibility of broadcasting in video. This may well resolve some of the issues, but any church considering going down this route needs to be very clear about its purpose in doing so.

CHAPTER 8

Technology and Ministry

As I've been saying all along, once you start down the technology route you will be continually looking (I hope) to see how you can improve. What software can you buy that will make your presentations more smooth or dramatic? What extra kit can you purchase to make the whole service seem more professional? Hopefully you will always be looking to do just that little bit better next time.

A technology ministry is for life ... not just for Christmas. But, from whom do you learn?

The learning process

The first place you learn is from your mistakes. I never mind when people make mistakes (I make enough of my own, after all) provided they use it as a learning experience. If the same mistakes are continually repeated then that clearly becomes a different matter. But, we all know, and it is true, that it is our mistakes that we learn from. The simplest of things can trip us up. A few years ago, I gave a cue to run a video at an Assembly. The operator pressed the button but nothing happened. I gave the cue again. He pressed the button again – still nothing. Then somebody looked over and casually suggested that it would work better if we actually put the video into the machine! Now, we know to check these things **before** the sessions start.

The other place to learn is obviously from others. This is where 'team' is important. You need to be able to visit other churches on Sundays to see how others are using technology. So, make sure you have somebody to hand over to on occasions. Nor restrict yourself to other churches. The secular world has much to teach us. I try to attend 'live' theatre on a fairly regular basis. Whether the performance is any good or not often passes me by: I'm too busy looking at the lighting rig. How are they using the lights? What lights are they using? What difference does using colour scrollers on the lights make? What effects are used? How are they done?

Look at the sets. What have they used? Sometimes going to smaller theatres can teach you more. Small theatres often put on productions with fairly minimalist sets. I've seen plays that have used little more than fabric backdrops, different levels of stage and one or two props. But, they've generated as much atmosphere, particularly with effective use of lights, as much bigger theatres with expensive sets.

If you attend conferences, look at how it is staged. Big companies, staging events, often have large budgets to work with. But they will probably be using the same basic material as your church – computers running PowerPoint® presentations, cameras, sound desk, etc. Look at how they use the equipment.

Rather than envy the big churches' or secular organisations' facilities and staff, use them to draw inspiration from what they do. Perhaps you are in a big church. Even the big churches can learn from the smaller ones. I was surprised to learn that the head of the audio-visual services at Willow Creek had visited North Coast Community Church in Vista, California. The latter church is very small by Willow Creek standards but they still had some different ideas that Willow Creek felt they could learn from. Never be too proud to learn from others.

Working as a team

Teams are important! The lesson to learn is – don't try to do it all yourself! It's always very tempting to think that only we know how to use the technology to best effect. But part of using our gifting is the sharing of knowledge with others. Working in a team can also stimulate creativity. Team discussions will often lead to a greater adrenaline rush and the much better flow of ideas.

Teamwork is important to the success of your ministry. Unless you plan to be at church every Sunday, for all services, fifty-two weeks of the year you will need to build a team around you. There are bound to be people – particularly young people –

who are keen to be part of the team. It is true that the Church's greatest resource is its people. But people need nurturing. A sense of team needs to be built, it doesn't just happen overnight. There will be people with different levels of expertise and different viewpoints! But everybody is important and you need to know their strengths and weaknesses. Know who needs that little extra bit of encouragement each week.

A team is able to support each other, in all kinds of ways. At the most practical level, a team can help each other put equipment away after use. There is nothing worse than being the last person left still tidying away kit, long after everybody else has departed for their Sunday lunch.

Being part of a team also allows for emotional support. When somebody on the team does a good job, other members should be prepared to acknowledge it. When things aren't going well, the team can offer support and guidance. However, the team must never become embroiled in a 'them and us' situation. Remember that the team's first task is to serve the whole church ministry. Don't allow the team to become a clique. Allow new people to join it. Ensure that there is a good relationship between the team and the church leadership. Be prepared to accept criticism from non-team members – if it is fair. Whilst being prepared to accept criticism, I do believe there are times when some criticism needs (perhaps deserves) to be challenged.

There are times when people who do the criticising don't perhaps realise the harm they can do, particularly to sensitive creative types. How often do we do something that ninety-nine people tell us is fantastic but one person tells us is rubbish? How much notice do we take of that one person? Too much! But, it is hard for creative types to keep this kind of thing in perspective. Criticism hurts. We put our heart and soul into presentations and perform-ances that are very public. Then one person who perhaps did not appreciate our performance knocks us down. Try to keep a sense of perspective. Take your concerns to the team. Talk it through. Pray it through. Was the criticism justified? If so, think about making adjustments. If it wasn't, you might want to think about the correct way to challenge that person. It may not be you who should do the challenging. It may need to be the pastor. But, don't allow it to eat away at you forever. Deal with it.

Make sure that all the team have a copy of the Mission Statement. You might want to have a copy of it visible on the production desk. A nice touch might be for all team members to sign it as a visible commitment to the ministry of the technical team.

Within a well-developed team there is room for critique and evaluation. Constructive critic-ism is always easier to handle amongst a group that is prepared to support and encourage one another. It is also the place where training can take place. If you can spend time together outside of the pres-surised atmosphere of the Sunday service or event where you are working hard to get things right, take time out for training. This need not mean attending expensive training courses. In my small team at work we quickly realised that we each had different skills that were not shared by all members of the team. In a small team this can have serious consequences if somebody is off sick, or just away on holiday. So, we took time out to share our skills with each other.

Take time out to ensure that everybody on the team knows their role. Take time also to pray together before a service. The importance of a happy technical team that knows what it is doing can not be stressed enough. At the 2001 Assembly in Blackpool, forty minutes before the start of each evening session the technical crew downed their headsets and met together. Although everybody had a copy of a full technical running order it gave every member of the team an opportunity to ask for clarification on anything they were unclear about. Even more importantly, it provided us with an opportunity to pray together. After all, the worship band, the speakers and other participants all meet beforehand and pray together – so why not the technical team?

You might want to have regular meetings of the technical team. These could take different forms:

○ Prayer and bible study. (I put this first as it is the most important!)
○ Training.
○ Checking equipment (take time to look after your equipment).
○ Review and evaluation sessions and forward planning.

○ Having fun! This might include trips to the theatre or concerts (to see how others do it … perhaps a bit of a 'busman's holiday'!)

The role of producers

Inevitably as the use of technology grows in the church so you will need to develop the team. There will be the sound engineer(s), a computer operator, a video operator and somebody else to operate the lights (even if this only means switching main lights on and off at any given time). If your church is broadcasting services and/or events on the Web somebody will need to be tasked with ensuring the live link is up and running the whole time and will need to be competent to restore the link if it is lost. Once the team begins to grow like this you might want to consider adding somebody to the role of producer.

Now, the term 'producer' might sound a bit Hollywoodish! But, realistically, this person will be responsible for ensuring that everything happens at the right time. At North Coast Community Church, Vista (see Case Study on p 67) each technical team has a producer. There are three main tasks for the team in the satellite services to remember – the sound, the lighting (the stage lights are switched off once the video feed of the main sermon begins) and the 'live' camera feed and/or video recording of the sermon has to be started. Not a great deal to remember you might think. But, in the slightly more pressurised atmosphere of a worship service it is easy for something to be overlooked.

One Sunday morning in the Video Café the video tape operator ran the video of the sermon and the sound engineer opened the fader. The congregation was momentarily mystified. The image on the screen and the sound were definitely not synchronised. Unfortunately, the sound engineer had opened the fader to the sound in the main sanctuary. The congregation were now hearing the preacher giving the message live in the main sanctuary but watching a video of the same preacher, giving the same message, but filmed at the Saturday night service. As the Video Café service was running at about five minutes behind the main service the congregation had every right to be mystified!

The mistake was quickly rectified as the sound engineer cross-faded between the live feed from the sanctuary to the sound for the video. All became much clearer!

It is at moments like these that the role of producer is thrown sharply into focus. It needs to be somebody who knows what is supposed to happen and can keep a cool head, helping the team to work together.

Team leadership

It might be that the producer becomes the team leader, or it may be somebody else entirely. Either way, somebody needs to be in charge. The team leader needs to ensure that services are thought through, material is produced, and that the team are assigned roles and know their responsibilities. But, more than that, the team leader must take responsibility for ensuring the well-being of the team. Remember – a projector can be insured and replaced if it goes wrong, but a person is priceless.

It will be the team leader's task to ensure that team members are affirmed, respected, trained and loved for who they are, not for what they do.

Caring for yourself spiritually

Every Sunday you are there, you make sure the technology works, pressing the buttons, pushing faders, ensuring that everything happens in a co-ordinated way. But at the end of the day – how much of the service have you actually heard?

We hold a post-mortem after every Assembly. After the 2001 Assembly my biggest concern was that I had barely heard a word of any address, Bible study or talk. With a different earpiece in each ear, connected to different radio channels, and sixteen people to co-ordinate there was always something happening. The opportunity to be spiritually blessed, as many are, is missed.

Just to make matters worse, I often find myself attending services or events wondering about the technical issues that are involved in the production. So, I might be sitting in a church service agonising over the poor sound, or the 'blank' screen. Or, I might be spellbound by a presentation and am busily taking notes as to how it has been produced.

This is a problem familiar to the techie. It's easy to get so involved in what we are doing that we do miss out on the heart of the service. Yet, Bill Hybels says, 'My ministry is the product of my relationship with Christ.'

Spending time spiritually preparing is as important as spending time creatively preparing. Taking time out for yourself is also valid. The danger is that creating so obsesses us, we get so tied up with deadlines, we never take time to step back and look at what it is we are doing. It's why ministers are allowed a sabbatical period. It enables them to step back, be refreshed, look again at what it is they are doing. Now, I'm not suggesting that you drop everything for three months! But, some time away, in a different environment, is no bad thing.

Remember that your technical and/or creative ability is a gift from God. Like all gifts it requires cherishing and nurturing. Don't take it for granted.

I've already argued that the techie has as much of a ministry as the worship leader or the preacher. What you do can help lead people to Christ. So, you need to be in as much of an attitude of worship as all the other artists/leaders in the church. Let me recommend a book to you. Rory Noland is the Music Director at Willow Creek and he has written a superb book called *The Heart of the Artist*. In it he talks about all the problems that confront the artist – our ability to become emotional at times, the difficulties of holding a team of artists together, facing up to criticism. But, he also gives very practical advice for overcoming the difficulties and for working with others to produce inspired worship with God at its centre.

How else might we use the technology?

I've written mostly about using the technology during church worship services. But, once you have the technology in place and the ability to use it well, you will find that it can be used in many different ways and places.

Jean Smith at Milton Baptist Church reports that they use the technology 'outside of services, too, such as suppers, mission evenings, members meetings, Alpha courses, flower shows, conferences, open days, film shows, plays and other productions.'

Also, does the outside of your church inspire people to walk through the door? What does your church noticeboard look like? Do you even have one? Does it give people the information they need? Does it tell them when the services are? What kind of service is it? Does it say who the minister(s) is (are)? Does it give a good impression? Is it fading? Is the paintwork peeling? If it's one of those large 'Day-Glo' posters – is it stuck down securely? Is everything spelt correctly?

Milton Baptist Church in are considering experimenting with an electronic noticeboard that can be updated regularly and which will give the impression of a dynamic, up-to-date church that knows what it is about.

There are other ways of using technology!

A cautionary tale

Before we finish, here's a cautionary tale written by my co-producer at the Baptist Assembly, Andy Voyce. So, before you all dash off to compile your equipment requirements and rush down to PC World to fill your church with all the latest technology – read on ...

Fred looked out on his congregation one Sunday morning, and what he saw both cheered and disheartened him. For sure there were the same faithful attenders, but it appeared that as he preached each week his words fell on deaf ears and failed to inspire and, to be honest, on most occasions seemed to fail to keep them awake!

After the service he went to the door as usual and received the weekly compliments on the 'Nice service this morning Vicar' time after time. In his frustration at the bland comments he questioned some on what they thought was the most important message that morning, and received back some rather vague replies. In his frustration he turned to his elder Dave and shared his despair with him. Dave did his best to console him and offered a few words of advice. You see, Dave had recently visited a church that used lots of new technology in their service, and so he shared his experience with Fred. Almost immediately Dave saw the light bulb of inspiration appear over Fred's head.

Monday morning came and Fred was the first through the doors of his local Computer mega-store, armed of course with a portion of the church budget. Through the week he begged and borrowed equipment and resources and worked frantically day and night in his garage.

Fred even managed to find the pairs of 3-D glasses off the back of his favourite Weetabix packets, that had so inspired him back in 1989 that he had brought 58 packs .... which he had almost finished!!

The following Sunday morning came around, and Fred was down to the church nice and early to set up for the service. Reg the PA man also had to come down early to set up the mixing desk that he had borrowed, as to Reg's surprise Fred had informed him that the usual two channels would not be enough this week. The congregation began to arrive and each was issued with their 3-D glasses. And as 10.30 drew closer there was an expectant buzz in the church and the adrenaline was really starting to flow through Fred.

10.30 came and the service began. Fred had titled the mornings service 'U2 can be like Christ' inspired of course by the content of the service ... and a video of a U2 concert that his son Jonathon had showed him on Wednesday of that week.

What ensued was nothing short of amazing! For the next 90 minutes that followed there were on-screen visuals, lights, video, links to the web, and a whole host of technology that touched the senses of the pew fillers. The children sang along to the latest Veggietales video and the adults gazed in awe as they donned their 3-D glasses and watched extracts from the latest BBC programme 'Jesus as he saw it', profiling the life of Jesus through the actual eyes of Jesus on the 'Jesuscam'!

They had songs on the big screen using random transitions. Fred had never seen the congregation move so much in worship, and as the lines flew in from the left right top and bottom of the screen during the songs and Fred's interactive sermon, he looked out on the congregation as they swayed and wowed with each line. So effective was this that when Fred flew in the word Saviour from big screen centre up to a staggering 224 point size, Mrs Perkins in the front row fell over backwards. What was even more worrying was that Mr Perkins thought Betty had been slain in the spirit.

There were lights, there was action ... and the cameras would come next week.

At the end of the service Fred went to the door as usual, and this week he was met with excited members who all thought this week's service was fantastic!!! Some liked the Jesus programme, others liked the readings on screen and the children loved the sing-a-long songs. So thrilled was Fred that he asked them again what they thought was the most important message of the morning. They replied again some liked the Jesus programme others liked the readings on screen and the children loved the sing-a-long songs. Suddenly it started to dawn on Fred that just like last week no one could actually tell him what the message was. And even though this week they were more enthusiastic, the situation had remained unchanged.

In his despair he turned to Dave the elder. 'Dave,' he said, 'where in the world did I go wrong?' Dave turned and said, 'Fred, where in the world, PC World.'

You see what Fred had failed to realise was that if the communication becomes about the technology itself, then the message is lost. Whilst technology when used well can enhance and reinforce the message, it cannot replace the message itself. We need to think creatively about what's available, and think constructively as to how it supports what we are trying to communicate. Because when it does work, it will inspire generations who are switched on to new media and who engage with personal stories.

Appendix

Useful addresses

Copyright licensing

Christian Copyright Licensing (Europe) Ltd
PO Box 1339
Eastbourne
East Sussex BN21 1AD
Tel: 01323 417711
Fax: 01323 417722
E-mail: info@ccli.co.uk
Web: www.ccli.co.uk

Performing Rights Society (PRS)
29/33 Berners Street
London W1P 4AH
Enquiries: 08000 684828
Tel: 0207 580 5544
Fax: 0207 306 4455
E-mail: musiclience@prs.co.uk
Web: www.prs.co.uk

The Copyright Licensing Agency Ltd
90 Tottenham Court Road
London W1P 0LP
Tel: 0207 631 5555
Fax: 0207 631 5500
E-mail: cla@cla.co.uk
Web: www.cla.co.uk

Mechanical Copyright Protection Society Ltd
29/33 Berners Street
London W1P 4AH
Tel: 0208 769 4400
Fax: 0208 378 7300
E-mail: info@mcps.co.uk
Web: www.mcps.co.uk

Phonographic Performance Ltd (PPL)
1 Upper James Street
London W1R 3HG
Tel: 0207 534 1030
Fax: 0207 534 1363
E-mail: GLD.info@ppluk.com
Web: www.ppluk.com

Resource providers

Willow Creek Association - UK
PO Box 622
Maidenhead SL6 0YX
Tel: 01628 620 602
Willow Creek Resources: 0800 592 083

Email: wcauk@aol.com
Web: www.willowcreek.org

Reaching The Unchurched Network (RUN)
PO Box 387
Aylesbury
Bucks HP21 8WH
Tel: 01926 334 242 or 0870 7873 635
E-mail: info@run.org.uk
Web: www.run.org.uk

Equipment and software providers

Sound Foundation
Unit A4
Acre Business Park
Acre Road
Reading
Berkshire RG2 0SA
Tel: 0118 986 6566
E-mail: sales@soundfoundation.com
Web: www.soundfoundation.com

Cunnings (for audio, visual and software require-
ments)
Cunnings Recording Associates
Brodrick Hall
Brodrick Road
London SW17 7DY
Tel: 020 8767 3533
E-mail: cunnings@compuserve.com

Reelife (importers of software)
Reelife Recordings
Laverick Hall
Halton
Lancaster LA2 6PH
Tel: 01524 811 282
E-mail: reelife@charis.co.uk